GROW

MARIJUANA INDOORS

*How to Have Personal Cultivation and Become an
Expert on Horticulture, Access the Secrets to
Grow Top-Shelf Buds, Marijuana Growing
Secrets, Cannabis, CBD And THC*

ANDERIA ZETTA ANDREW PAULL

TABLE OF CONTENTS

Introduction

This book will teach you everything you need to know about marijuana, cannabis, indoor gardening, etc. Before we begin, we will take some time to ensure that we are all on the same page regarding cannabis and marijuana knowledge basics. That way, you will be ready to dive into the rest of the book with a solid understanding of the foundational concepts related to marijuana.

What This Book Will Teach You

In this book, I will ensure that you learn and understand the growing and producing marijuana. We will delve into marijuana, including how to care for and understand your plants, what kinds of marijuana plants you can grow, how to avoid pests and disease in your garden, and how to use marijuana to benefit your life. I will also teach you the different options available to you for growing your marijuana plants indoors and some of the things you will need to keep in mind as you begin to grow plants of your own. By the end of this book, you will be ready to benefit from your indoor marijuana garden!

What Is Marijuana?

Marijuana is something that everybody knows about, but that few understand in-depth. As someone who wants to grow marijuana plants of their own, learning as much as you can about marijuana will benefit you. It will help you understand your plants and get the highest yield possible. Marijuana is the main topic that we will be discussing throughout this book, and we will explore it in-depth over the next several chapters. Before moving on, I will define the term *marijuana* for you.

Marijuana is a term used to describe a type of plant. This plant species has gained immense popularity in the media and politics over the past century. We have seen a drastic increase over the last fifty years, particularly in its global attention. The marijuana plant boasts several medicinal benefits and its intoxicating ones, which is why it has become so popular in recent years.

Marijuana is the name given to the dried leaves, seeds, stems, and flowers of the cannabis plant. This plant can come in many different forms, and there are many different ways to use these forms.

The reason that marijuana is so popular amongst young people is that the consumption of this dried flower leads to the feeling of being "high." Marijuana can be consumed either by inhalation, ingestion, or topical application. For this reason, the government classifies this as a banned substance in much of the world. We characterize a *high* by the following effects: pleasant feelings of relaxation, euphoria, and fatigue.

Marijuana vs. Cannabis vs. Hemp

We often use the terms *cannabis, marijuana,* and *hemp* interchangeably. It is still necessary to understand the differences between the three as we move forward in this book. By understanding this distinction, you will fully grasp the topics in each chapter of this book. In this section, I will outline the differences between Cannabis, Hemp, and Marijuana for you.

Hemp and marijuana are two different forms of the Cannabis plant. Marijuana is what most people speak about when they use casual or "street" terms such as *weed, pot,* or *Mary Jane.* Marijuana is the type of cannabis that includes significant amounts of the compound THC, which we will learn about in this book's first chapter.

Hemp, however, is a different form of cannabis. Hemp is different from marijuana in its THC content. THC is the psychoactive chemical in cannabis responsible for giving people a *high* feeling when they smoke or ingest it.

Hemp is the form of cannabis that contains less than 0.3% THC. Hemp is still cannabis, but that it does not have significant levels of psychoactivity when consumed. Since it is THC that is responsible for the effects known as a *high, hemp does not lead to a high.* Thus, we most often use hemp for things like clothing and medicinal purposes, among other things.

Throughout this book, I will use the word *cannabis* when speaking about the plant in a general sense. I will use the word *marijuana* when talking about the plant's form as a recreational drug.

A History of Marijuana

Knowing where the marijuana came from and how people first discovered it could help us to understand how it developed into the multi-million-dollar industry that it is today. We will begin by looking at where humans first found it and where it came from before delving deeper into its history.

Cannabis grows in the wild in a variety of regions across the world. It is challenging to trace marijuana back to a specific location, time, or use. Still, scientists are hard at work trying to determine the exact origins of this beautiful plant. As a result of recent scientific investigation of fossil pollen, scientists suspect that marijuana originally comes from the Tibetan Plateau. The fossils that led scientists to draw this conclusion demonstrate that the marijuana plant's origins date back to this location in northwestern China, somewhere around 19.6 million years ago. They then began to determine that this plant traveled to Europe 6 million years ago and then to China's eastern side 1.2 million years ago. Scientists have also found it growing in the northern regions of Pakistan. There, people have seen it reach heights comparable to the first story of a high-rise building! These wild cannabis plants do not contain very high levels of the chemical responsible for the psychoactive effects of consuming cannabis, so it was not used as a recreational drug until much later.

At the beginning of its use by humans, marijuana (cannabis) was used as an herbal medicine instead of a recreational drug and getting high. These first uses of marijuana date back to somewhere around 500 BC. These first uses are said to have been somewhere in the central region of the continent of Asia. Back in that time, the marijuana plant was harvested in the wild and grown to be used by humans to treat pain relief, herbal medicine, and other herbal medicine uses.

The Chinese Emperor, Shen Nung, was responsible for the oldest record of marijuana use in written form. This writing was in 2727 BC. This instance could be the first discovery of marijuana, though it is challenging to say. There is also evidence that the first uses of marijuana were by ancient people who resided on the Tibetan Plateau in China. These people used marijuana during funerals on this mountain plateau. They did so because people who were nearby when it was burning reported feeling intoxicating properties. This theory is further evidenced by discovering burned marijuana seeds in shamans graves, as mentioned in the previous section. Later, Chinese farmers began to grow marijuana purposefully to take advantage of its many possible uses.

Over time, marijuana showed that it had many more uses than merely medicinal pain relief. This plant continued to be grown intentionally for some time. Eventually, it was then introduced into the ecosystems of Africa and Europe so that these regions could benefit from this plant.

These original strains of marijuana plants were only mildly psychoactive. This mild psychoactivity could be why people primarily used it for purposes other than as a recreational drug. Some researchers believe that the ancient peoples who used these plants for their medicinal purposes knew about the psychoactive potential of marijuana. Still, there is more evidence supporting the fact that this was not its primary use. Some researchers believe that ancient cultures intentionally developed and grew different hemp plants strains, leading them to develop plants containing higher levels of the psychoactive components within marijuana, called THC (which we will look at in-depth later in this book).

While the first reported recreational uses of marijuana are much more recent than its first discovery, the plant grew and thrived in nature well before humans existed, let alone discovered it. When humans came upon it, they decided to begin using it for their own medicinal and recreational purposes, though it had been around much longer than them.

The first reported uses of marijuana in America were somewhere around its colonization, somewhere around 1492. Reportedly, this was when it began to be grown and cultivated in this part of the world. In colonial times in America, farmers were responsible for developing and harvesting marijuana plants. Since it is a plant that grows quickly and is versatile and resilient, this plant could be grown and harvested in large quantities at a time. Eventually, this became the only way that marijuana was allowed to be grown, at least in the colonies around Connecticut, Massachusetts, and Virginia around the 1600s.

Compared to Asia, the difference in this part of the world is that the marijuana plant was grown to be used for fabric and textiles and make rope, not for medicinal purposes. In the Americas, people grew the hemp plant and made it useful for clothing, paper, and even food. People began to understand that the hemp plant seeds were edible and a great source of protein, vitamins, and minerals. After its introduction in the Americas, marijuana gained a lot of attention and became controversial for racial and political reasons. As marijuana was introduced and then later controlled, there were very significant race issues within the United States. These issues of the race eventually led to the criminalization of marijuana in the USA. This illegality remains today in the vast majority of states within the USA.

In 1937, there was something called the Marijuana Tax Act of 1937, a law created by the federal government that was put into place to criminalize marijuana in the United States. Further, this law placed a tax on the sale and the possession of any hemp product. This Marijuana Tax Act limited the production and distribution of marijuana to industrial companies and uses only and began the punishment of anyone found with marijuana for any other uses. One day after the Tax Act came into effect, a farmer got charged with the sale of marijuana, and he got a sentence of 4 years of punishment for this action. His punishment included hard labor of a variety of sorts.

Before World War II, with the growing of hemp in some regions of the United States, there was a tremendous import of hemp from the Philippines. After World War II, however, the Philippines was devastated by Japanese armed forces, and the United States had to rely on its domestic production and harvest of hemp plants to continue the sale for industrial purposes. In 1957, the United States had its final legal hemp field planted in Wisconsin. The demand for hemp declined severely after the second World War.

The War On Drugs began in 1970, when Richard Nixon, the United States president, decided to abolish the Marijuana Tax Act. He also decided to list marijuana as a Schedule 1 drug from then on. Other drugs included in the Schedule 1 category had heroin, ecstasy, and LSD. Under this new Controlled Substances Act of 1970, Richard Nixon deemed marijuana a drug that lacked any medical uses, which carried a high potential for drug abuse. They considered it a "gateway drug," meaning that it was considered a drug that would lead people to other, more severe drug addictions or drug abuse such as heroin or cocaine.

After the War on Drugs began in 1970, a report two years later mentioned that marijuana might not be the evil drug that the government made it out to be two years prior. This report was put forth by the National Commission on Marijuana and Drug Abuse, and it deemed marijuana as a misunderstood drug. This report stated the recommendation for less severe sentences related to the possession or the sale of marijuana. The president ignored this report, and the War on Drugs continued.

The state of California put forth the Compassionate Use Act in 1996, which decriminalized the use of marijuana by those who wished to use it to deal with chronic disease and illness. Following this, 26 other states and Washington, D.C., and Puerto Rico and Guam (which are territories of the USA), also legalized marijuana use for people with chronic and severe illnesses.

In 2019, Canada legalized the recreational use of marijuana across the entire country. It became the largest country to do so, the second entire nation to do so, after Uruguay, which did so in 2013. There was quite a gap between these two monumental moments in the legalization of marijuana.

The history of marijuana is wrought with controversy. To this day, there are still many conflicting opinions on this plant. Throughout the remainder of this book, we will explore many aspects of marijuana, including the medicinal properties, how it can be used and benefitted from recreationally, and how the future of marijuana looks. Read through this book with an open mind. You will discover for yourself how you can benefit from this beautiful plant full of possibilities for anyone, no matter what they are looking to get out of it.

Marijuana Facts

- Other Names for Cannabis

Many names are floating around in the world for marijuana, and they all mean the same thing. Here, we will discuss some of the names for marijuana to ensure we are all on the same page as we begin this book. You may have heard various slang terms for cannabis before and not even known that these names were about cannabis. Here, we will bring them all to once place.

The following names for cannabis are the proper terms found in more scientific writing or the plant's discussion.

- Marijuana
- Hashish
- Hemp
- Dagga
- Ganja

The following names are slang terms for the marijuana plant.

- 420
- Devil's Lettuce
- Mary Jane
- M.J.
- Reefer
- Harsh- A term to describe cannabis of poor-quality
- Flower
- Hash
- Kief- A name to describe cannabis of good quality
- Bud
- Herb
- Weed
- Pot
- Cryptonite

- Ace
- Chronic
- Grass
- Bhang

You have probably heard people using many of these names to describe cannabis in the past, and some of them may be new to you. Just know that all of these names mean the same thing: the cannabis plant in some form or another.

- The marijuana plant is a weed.

The cannabis plant can withstand a wide range of temperature conditions, water levels, and other weather-related variables. It is a very sturdy and resilient plant, which is likely why one of its nicknames is "weed." Weeds are notoriously pesky plants that keep coming back once you remove them from your garden and seem to withstand virtually any weather conditions.

- Marijuana is the number one most used drug across the world.

- Marijuana is versatile

Marijuana affects just about every one of your organs, which is one of the reasons why it is so versatile. For this reason, people enjoy marijuana for so many different reasons.

- Marijuana contains over 120 chemicals.

There are so many different marijuana strains because the cannabis plant contains more than 120 various chemical components, which can vary in amount, and all have slightly different properties. They, therefore, affect the user in different ways when consumed.

- Cannabis grows in the wild.

You can sometimes find cannabis growing in the wild if you are lucky enough to stumble upon it. You can find this plant growing naturally (without being planted by humans) in the Himalayas, India, Nepal, Pakistan, China, and Asia. However, the tricky part about it is that we most often find it in these mountain tops' remote corners where humans rarely venture or venture with ease. Some farmers in these regions can assist in the cannabis plant's growth and then live on their crops. When authorities ask, they must claim that their cannabis crops are naturally grown since they are native to these regions because they are ruled illegal by their governments.

Now that you understand what marijuana is and a brief history of it, the rest of this book will teach you exactly how you can benefit from the many uses of this magical plant.

Chapter 1: The Science
of Marijuana

This chapter will look a little deeper into the science of marijuana and learn about what makes this plant so fascinating to humans. By learning more about the science behind this plant, you will understand how it can benefit you and the mechanisms by which this happens in your body. This chapter will also help you to understand why this plant is loved and cherished by so many.

The Components of Marijuana

As I touched on in the introduction to this book, different chemicals within the cannabis plant are responsible for giving people the good feelings that have made marijuana and cannabis in general so well known. In this section, we are going to learn about these chemicals and how they affect a person.

There are two primary components of the cannabis plant. These chemicals are responsible for making cannabis such a desirable drug and therapy for many people today. These two chemicals are; *THC,* which stands for *tetrahydrocannabinol,* and *CBD*, which stands for *cannabidiol.* These two chemicals act in different ways in the human body, and in this section, we will look at what makes them desirable when choosing a recreational drug.

What Is CBD?

CBD stands for *cannabidiol.* It is another chemical found in the cannabis plant, which can provide humans with various benefits. CBD and THC are often found together in the cannabis plant, though each can vary. This section will learn about CBD, and then we will look at THC in detail before comparing the similarities and differences between them.

We can find CBD in both varieties of cannabis- hemp and marijuana. THC does not come in significant amounts in hemp, but CBD is always in hemp. CBD provides the consumer with many different effects than THC does. There are many ways that a person can consume CBD without consuming THC if they do not want to get high.

CBD is a "nonpsychoactive" chemical, which means that it does not give the consumer any type of psychoactive effects when consumed. CBD can be consumed in large amounts with little to no side-effects, as it is **not** a psychoactive compound.

What Is THC?

THC, as you know by now, stands for tetrahydrocannabinol. This chemical is responsible for the effects known as the "high," those feelings of euphoria and relaxation that come from smoking or ingesting marijuana.

When a human consumes THC, it makes its way into the bloodstream. When THC reaches the bloodstream, it makes its way to the brain. Once there, it produces the effects known as the "high" because it finds receptors in the brain that it can attach itself to, which creates the high.

There are many ways to consume THC; the most common way is through the marijuana flower, which is how you will find it once you grow it on your own. We will look at how you can do this later on in this book.

THC comes with some side-effects in varying degrees, though these side-effects are temporary, meaning that they are present only for the duration of the high. These side-effects can include;

- An increase in heart rate
- Lowered coordination
- Memory impairment
- Dry mouth
- Red eyes
- A reduction in reaction time.

The side-effects that THC produces are a direct result of its psychoactive effects on the brain. When we talk about side effects, we mean the effects caused by the fact that THC is a psychoactive chemical. We will look

at the mechanisms by which this psychoactive chemical works in the brain later on in this chapter.

THC is not known to lead to death for any reason, but
it can lead to long-term psychiatric changes. These are
most commonly due to long-term use by adolescents
whose brains are still growing and developing.

Similarities and Differences between CBD and THC

It can be confusing to remember the differences between THC and CBD, so I have included a chart for
you that will help you to visualize and recognize the
differences and similarities between THC and CBD.

	CBD	THC
What kind of canna-bis plant does it come from?	Hemp and Marijuana	Marijuana
Illegal in Most Places	No	Yes
Gives the consumer a high	No	Yes
Side-Effects	No	Yes
Psychoactive?	No	Yes
Therapeutic Effects	Yes	Yes
Reduces Psychosis	Yes	No

The Benefits of CBD

CBD is known to help with the following, without leading to any sort of feeling of being "high;"

- Treatment for Anxiety and Depression

CBD is known to help treat anxiety and depression. It can help a person feel relaxed and at ease, which can be great for treating anxiety. It can also help treat depression by leading to feelings of being at peace with one's current situation. It does this by binding to receptors in the brain related to *serotonin* responsible for depression. Serotonin controls mood, which is why reduced amounts of it can cause depression. CBD's ability to act on the brain's serotonin receptors makes it a great natural alternative to regular pharmaceutical drugs. One of the benefits of using CBD as a treatment for anxiety and depression is that you will treat these illnesses without the side effects of pharmaceutical drugs prescribed to treat anxiety and depression. Further, some anxiety and depression medications can be addictive and are, therefore, dangerous due to developing substance abuse or dependency.

Some studies have been done on children with post-traumatic stress disorder (or PTSD) wherein they gave participants doses of CBD to help with the anxiety associated with this disorder. This study showed that CBD proved useful as a treatment for the stress related to PTSD in children.

Additionally, studies have shown that CBD acts very similarly to antidepressants in the brain. There have been studies on both humans and animals, and in both samples, CBD proved to be a very successful antidepressant.

- Treatment for Psychosis or Other Mental Health Conditions

Since CBD does not have any psychoactive effects, it is an excellent choice for those looking to deal with psychosis or any other mental health condition of this sort, such as schizophrenia. The relaxation and calm that CBD can provide a person with are beneficial in treating or improving psychosis. The same is not true for marijuana, which also contains significant amounts of THC. THC will not reduce psychosis; it will increase it. It is essential to be aware of your product's THC content before using it to treat psychosis.

- Reducing Insomnia

CBD is an effective treatment for insomnia in both children and adults. In these studies, CBD was useful for not only falling asleep but staying asleep as well. The reason for this is still unknown; however, the results are concrete. Some hypothesize that CBD can induce relaxation and feelings of calm in those who consume it, leading to better and more restful sleep. This improved sleep is because there are underlying causes for insomnia related to the mind and anxiety, so treating these underlying causes is the real way to treat insomnia.

One thing to note about using CBD for insomnia is that it usually will take some time for the results to begin taking action. These studies took somewhere around four weeks of regular consumption for patients to start noticing CBD's effects on their insomnia.

- Neuroprotection

CBD has neuroprotective effects in the brain. The word neuroprotective comes from the two words, *neuron* and *protection.* Neurons are cells in the brain that send signals, which creates our thoughts, our feelings, our movements, and virtually everything else that the body does. This process begins in the brain. CBD demonstrates the ability to protect neurons' structure in the brain, which prevents the loss and damage of neurons throughout a person's life due to injury and/ or aging. This benefit is not only helpful for people who wish to keep their brains healthy and robust but especially for those who suffer from neurological disorders such as multiple sclerosis (MS) and epilepsy. These disorders are related to neuronal dysfunction, and CBD effectively reduces the symptoms and the severity of these diseases. For example, CBD proves to reduce seizures in those with epilepsy. The research in this area is still in its infancy, but the results are promising.

- Addiction Treatment

Scientists are currently studying CBD as a treatment for addiction and substance abuse. CBD acts on the brain in areas specifically related to addiction and substance abuse. Thus, CBD is an effective treatment for reducing substance dependence and the behaviors and thoughts of addiction. This theory is heavily studied, and there is still much more information to come from these studies.

- Reducing Inflammation

CBD has been shown to reduce inflammation in the brain and other areas of the body. One such example is the role that CBD can play in reducing the severity and the progression of Alzheimer's disease. This benefit is because of its ability to reduce the inflammation in the brain associated with Alzheimer's and the degeneration of neurons in the brain that is part of dementia and Alzheimer's. This reduction of inflammation can help the person's condition remain stable and slow these diseases' decline.

- Pain Management and Reduction

Marijuana in various forms has been used as a treatment for pain for centuries since the first demonstrated uses in 2900 BC. One of the reasons why marijuana is so great for pain reduction is because of its CBD content. This benefit is because CBD acts in the brain and spinal cord. Once there, it binds to specific receptors associated with inflammation and sensations. CBD relieves pain in part by acting on the pain signals which travel from the site of pain to the brain, reducing your awareness of your pain- which is a large part of feeling pain. It does this by getting in the way of the pain signals to reach their target sites within the brain. Since

CBD also has relaxing and mood-boosting effects, it can help a person in pain take their mind off the bad and switch its focus to the positive, which can help relieve pain as it is not in the front of the person's mind.

There have been numerous studies that showed that CBD was an effective treatment for arthritis and Multiple Sclerosis. CBD is also used as a treatment for different pain types, though most studies have been done on individuals experiencing various chronic pain forms such as arthritis.

- Treatment for Inflammatory Bowel Disease

As you now know, CBD is an effective treatment for inflammation. For this reason, it is a great way to treat disorders associated with inflammation of different areas of the body, such as the bowels. Inflammatory Bowel Disease or IBD is a disease that can lead to pain and bloating as a result of an inflamed bowel. Irritable Bowel Syndrome or IBS is another example of this type of disorder. CBD is an effective treatment for these disorders as it reduces general inflammation in the body.

- Reducing Nausea

Nausea is relieved by the consumption of CBD. The mechanism by which this works is still widely unknown, but through numerous studies, it has shown to reduce both nausea and vomiting. In this way, it can help morning sickness, side-effects of cancer treatments, and just general nausea.

- Migraine Treatment

Since CBD is so useful for pain relief, this is an excellent option for those who suffer from migraines. These intensely painful headaches involve tense muscles of the neck and often bring about nausea and sometimes even vomiting. CBD will not only help to reduce the pain of a migraine, but it will also relieve nausea and vomiting associated with migraines.

- Treatment for Seizures

Since the brain functions by sending small electrical impulses back and forth along with its cells, the malfunction of these processes can cause various types— for example, seizures. Seizures happen due to a sort of "electrical storm" within the cells of the brain. This effect causes seizure symptoms, such as convulsions, abnormal behaving, and sometimes the loss of consciousness. Since CBD has proven to be neuroprotective- it protects the brain cells from damage and degeneration; it can help prevent seizures in people with epilepsy. Still, it can also reduce the risk of seizures in people who do not have epilepsy but run the risk of having a seizure for other reasons.

- Anti-Acne Benefits

Acne is a skin condition that affects many, many people. This condition is associated with producing an oil called *sebum* in the skin and inflammation in the skin's deeper layers. Since CBD reduces inflammation, it is an effective acne treatment. Further, CBD has shown to reduce sebum production in the skin, which also reduces acne. These studies used CBD in CBD oil, made from CBD extraction from the hemp plant, and mixed it with other natural oil such as hemp seed oil or coconut oil.

- Cancer Symptoms

There are several symptoms related to cancer and cancer treatments. These symptoms can include nausea, vomiting, pain, appetite loss, and so on. One study gave a combination of THC and CBD to cancer patients who had not been responding to regular pain medications, and this proved to reduce pain compared to people who got THC-only compounds.

It has also proven to reduce nausea and vomiting that is associated with chemotherapy and other cancer treatments. In some people, regular cancer medications are ineffective, and they seek alternatives to these. CBD and combinations of THC and CBD are effective alternatives to these drugs in many cases.

- Anti-Tumor

CBD has been shown through studies to be an anti-tumor agent. In studies on animal test subjects, CBD proved to prevent the spread of several cancers due to its anti-tumor effects. In one study, CBD showed to induce cell death in tumor cells in human women with breast cancer. In mice, a study tested a CBD concentrate in mice with breast cancer tumors, and this study resulted in the inhibition of the spread of these cancer cells in the mouse subjects. More studies are happening which test the effectiveness of this type of treatment in human subjects.

- Improves Heart Health

CBD has been shown to reduce blood pressure in patients with high blood pressure. In turn, this reduces a person's risk of diseases such as stroke, metabolic syndrome, and heart attacks as these conditions are associated with higher blood pressure.

CBD also helps to manage and reduce the symptoms of heart disease as it reduces the inflammation of the heart and can reduce the instances of heart cell death/ heart damage present in heart disease. This benefit is also thanks to its ability to lower stress levels and antioxidant properties.

- Diabetes Treatment

Diabetes is the misregulation of blood sugar due to problems with the hormone insulin. Treatment with CBD showed reductions in inflammation associated with diabetes, improving the related symptoms, and reducing the incidence of diabetes in mouse subjects.

The Benefits of THC

While many people consider the high feeling that THC gives them a positive element of consuming marijuana, many others do not benefit. In this section, we will look at the numerous other benefits that THC can provide a person with, aside from a feeling of being high.

THC helps with the following, in addition to the feeling of being "high;"

- Improves Insomnia

Marijuana use leads to fatigue, which makes it a good treatment for insomnia. Many people turn to marijuana to help them fall asleep each night. Further, because of the relaxation and euphoria that marijuana can lead to, this can help people suffering from insomnia to relax and fall asleep more easily.

- Reduces Stress

The euphoria associated with THC consumption can reduce stress as it helps people see things in a more positive light than they may have before consuming THC. Further, people's relaxation and fatigue when they consume cannabis are beneficial in reducing stress levels.

- Reduces Pain

THC is a proven remedy for all sorts of different pain that people may experience. THC first became accepted by governments solely for medicinal purposes, one of the primary goals being pain reduction.

For people suffering from chronic illnesses, consuming THC is a proven, natural method to relieve their pain. There are different strains of marijuana, each containing different levels of THC. These different strains are beneficial for various reasons and other types of pain, so people wishing to use THC for pain relief can begin to experiment with different strains depending on what they are looking for. There are three different types of pain that a person may experience. The first is called *nociceptive pain.* This type of pain is what a person would experience after some type of damage to the body. This kind of damage can include breaking an arm or having arthritis (since this results from inflammation and damage to the joints). The second type of pain is called *neuropathic pain,* and this type of pain is the type a person would experience as a result of nerve pain or nerve-related issues in their body.

An example of this could be carpal tunnel syndrome or any kind of nerve damage. The third and final type of pain is called *central pain.* Central pain is a type of pain that stems from the central nervous system, which includes the brain, the brainstem, and the spinal cord. This pain results from damage to one of these areas or a type of dysfunction in these areas. The problems that cause this pain can range from a stroke to brain trauma to a tumor to Parkinson's disease and fibromyalgia.

This type of pain is due to more severe issues since it involves the brain and the spinal cord. The kind of pain that you experience can determine the kind of remedy you need.

For nociceptive pain (injury pain), the pain happens because of damage to the body and the inflammation in that area that results. This inflammation occurs as a response to the damage, but it leads to pain and discomfort. To relieve this type of pain, you must target the inflammation. THC aids in reducing inflammation, which, in turn, reduces the pain associated with the injury. Further, the pain signals travel from the site of injury to the brain, where your brain interprets it as pain. THC also acts to slow or lessen the traveling of these pain signals to reduce a person's perception of their pain.

Neuropathic pain or pain associated with the body's nerves is the type of pain that arises from damage to the nervous system. This type of pain is most often caused by the pinching of nerves, which can cause damage eventually, the injury to a nerve, or by some kind of stabbing that causes nerve damage. The difference between this type of pain and nociceptive pain is that it does not involve inflammation, so it is difficult to treat with common drugs that usually target inflammatory cells. The reason that THC is such a beneficial treatment for this type of pain is that it leads to the reduction of pain in different ways than most pharmaceutical products do. THC leads to a decrease in pain related to nerve damage by protecting the nerve cells themselves and increasing the person's mood and feelings of positivity. These two effects, when combined, are powerful neuropathic pain relievers.

Central pain is a relatively new term as it is a relatively discovery in the science world. Central pain is tricky as it is present in the absence of any visible injury or any real source. Fibromyalgia is an example of this type of pain. Fibromyalgia is a sort of general pain that can be experienced all over the body. There is no root cause of fibromyalgia, and this is why it is an interesting field of study as of late. Scientists theorize that this disease is caused by dysfunction in how the brain processes pain signals. It is very difficult to find treatments for this type of pain, but THC has proven extremely beneficial. This benefit could be because it slows and dulls the pain signals as they travel to the brain or due to the mood change that accompanies THC consumption. The mechanisms of action on central pain, in particular, are still mostly unknown, but at this stage, it is an excellent option for treating this type of pain.

For example, a recent study conducted on people suffering from Multiple Sclerosis (MS) showed that treatment with THC led to a reduction in the pain that they regularly experienced due to muscle and joint stiffness and tightness as the nerve pain that they experience. People suffering from MS experience recurring nerve pain as their nerve cells lose their protective coating. This lack of protection leaves the nerve cells exposed and causes the person pain at the nerve-level.

- Reduces Nausea

It is not entirely understood why yet, but THC consumption is proven to reduce nausea. This nausea reduction can be beneficial for various reasons, such as those going through chemotherapy or who suffer from nausea for any other reason.

- Treatment for Muscle Spasticity

Muscle Spasticity is the presence of involuntary muscle contractions that lead to spasms. These spasms can happen for various reasons that are not too serious, but it can become a recurring problem for some people. In these individuals, much of the time, the treatment includes some combination of anti-inflammatory drugs, anti-anxiety medications, muscle relaxants, and other prescribed drugs such as these. The great thing about marijuana is that it produces all of these effects in one.

Instead of turning to a cocktail of prescribed pharmaceuticals, one can achieve all of these effects from a single treatment using marijuana.

- Treatment for Glaucoma

Glaucoma is a medical condition that involves damage to the main nerve in the eye for some reason. This damage is usually due to genetics, and it can progress to a point where a person experiences vision loss or even blindness. Blindness can happen because of an increase in eye pressure, which eventually damages the *optic nerve*. The optic nerve, the main nerve within the eye, is responsible for sending visual messages from the eye to the brain to be interpreted. If these messages cannot reach the brain, a person will lose the ability to see as the visual messages cannot reach their brain.

Marijuana consumption in patients with Glaucoma reduces pressure within the eye, preventing further damage to the optic nerve, preventing damage that has already occurred from getting worse, and reducing the risk of developing lasting damage due to high-pressure levels within the eye.

One of the reasons this is still a new area of study within the medical research community is that the side effects of THC consumption must be considered in these patients, as they would need to be consuming THC every four hours. They would need to do this because the pressure reduction in the eye caused by THC only lasts for roughly four hours. This frequency is not very practical. If there can be new ways to develop Glaucoma treatments based on THC research, this could be a new research area and innovation for those suffering from Glaucoma.

- Treatment for Low Appetite

THC leads to an increase in appetite, commonly known as "the munchies." This increase in appetite can be extremely beneficial for those with eating disorders or underweight people for any reason. This effect is also beneficial for those who are getting cancer treatments and have a reduced appetite.

- Migraine Reduction

THC's pain relief effects help people who suffer from migraines, as many over-the-counter pain relief treatments prove to be ineffective at treating migraines.

- Reducing Inflammation

THC is a very effective treatment for reducing inflammation throughout the body.

The Science Of How We Use Marijuana

In this section, we will break the science of marijuana down to consumption, which will affect how the body processes the chemicals, leading to different kinds of benefits and different highs.

Inhalation through Smoking

We will begin by looking at the mechanism by which marijuana acts when you inhale it into your lungs by smoking. When you smoke marijuana, the THC that we just learned about it absorbed into the bloodstream through the thin layers in your lungs. Once THC enters your bloodstream in this way, it begins to give you the therapeutic effects that you seek. It does this by making its way through your bloodstream to your brain. Once the THC gets to your bloodstream, it will make its way to your brain in just seconds.

Smoking marijuana is the quickest way to feel the effects of a marijuana-induced high. It is also the most common way to consume marijuana. Within the lungs, there are millions of small pockets of air. This location is where air exchange occurs whenever you inhale- the clean air goes into the bloodstream, and the used air goes into the lungs, which then exhale it into the atmosphere. When you inhale air filled with marijuana smoke, the gas exchange that occurs moves the air containing THC and CBD into the bloodstream through these small pockets of air called *alveoli.* These pockets are responsible for passing THC into your system. The reason that inhaling marijuana is the quickest way to get high is that these small pockets of air are plentiful and thin layers of the membrane form them.

For this reason, the exchange of gas across these membranes happens very quickly. The other reason is that these alveoli lead the consumer to feel such a quick high because these alveoli have such a high surface area, and this surface area allows the lungs to absorb a lot of air quickly. Then, once this THC makes its way into the bloodstream with ease, it also quickly makes its way to the brain as it joins the regular stream of blood that is pumping its way through your body. Since this happens all day every day without your knowledge, your body is extremely efficient at processing the air you breathe in and passing it all around your body. When you add THC into this blood flow, the body is still just as efficient at passing it around.

Once the THC reaches the brain- seconds after it reaches the bloodstream, it begins changing the brain's chemistry. The most common initial feelings that marijuana use elicits are feelings of relaxation and light-headedness. This feeling is the feeling that many people enjoy and is what keeps them coming back to marijuana. After some time, the effects of marijuana consumption can change from relaxation to paranoia and anxiety. The results that a person feels and the extent to which they feel them are largely dependent on the strain of marijuana they consume, the amount they consume, how they consume it, and finally, the person themselves and their brain chemistry. We will discuss this concept in more depth later. In general, THC acts in the brain by impersonating the brain's chemicals, thereby interfering with the brain's regular operations.

There are specific spots within the brain where THC and CBD molecules can attach themselves. The areas where these spots are are responsible for learning, problem-solving, coordination, and short-term memory. This evidence may explain why you feel that these areas of your brain are affected when you smoke. For example, THC acts on the hippocampus, an area of the brain associated with short-term memory. When THC binds to the hippocampus receptors, it is difficult

for the brain to make new short-term memories. Another example of this is the cerebellum, an area of the
brain responsible for balance and coordination. When
THC binds to the receptors in this brain area, it is difficult for the cerebellum to control the body's coordination and balance.

Inhalation through Vaporizing

When using a vaporizer to inhale marijuana, marijuana
becomes heated enough for the active chemicals to become vapor. When your inhale this vapor, it works in
the same way as smoking does once in your lungs. The
main difference is that some people prefer to inhale vapor rather than smoke. When you use a vaporizer, the
marijuana isn't heated enough to burn it, and this is why
you inhale vapor instead of smoke.

Edibles

When consuming marijuana in the form of edibles, you
ingest it just like any other food. Edible is usually made
by baking oil from the marijuana plant into something
like a cookie or drinking it in tea. Once you eat the edibles, they enter your digestive system through your
mouth and make their way to your stomach. Once they
enter your stomach, the bloodstream absorbs the THC

through the walls of your digestive system. Once in your bloodstream, the THC makes its way to your brain in the same way that it does in the above methods, leading to the feeling of being high.

The difference between ingesting marijuana through edibles and inhaling it through smoking is in the absorption of THC. This method is where you can see clear differences and form preferences regarding your methods of choice. As I mentioned, when you inhale marijuana through smoke, the absorption of THC is very quick because of the large surface area and thin membranes of the alveoli. When you ingest it by way of edibles, however, your body absorbs the THC much slower. This delay happens because the stomach is much slower at absorbing. The membranes are thicker, and there is less surface area for absorption. However, some people choose edibles over inhalation because while the effects of the high take longer to come on, they last much longer than they would through inhalation.

Chapter 2: The Basics of the Marijuana Plant

Throughout this chapter, we are going to look at the uses of marijuana. This chapter will give you a great introduction to the various uses for the marijuana plants that you plan to grow on your own! As you will find out through reading this chapter, the possibilities are endless.

Other Ways to Use Marijuana

In the previous chapter, we looked at the science behind different forms of consuming marijuana. In this section, we will be exploring the numerous ways that you can use marijuana in much more depth. The most popular way that is portrayed by the media is to smoke marijuana through the use of a joint. Although this is a common and frequently practiced method, you can use other ways to use marijuana. First of all, you don't always need to smoke it. You can ingest it as well through making food or drinks with it. Each type of method will provide you with a different high sensation, and everyone has their preference.

Moreover, if you need to use marijuana for specific purposes, this chapter will help you decide which one is best for you. For instance, if you are an athlete and can't compromise your lung functions, but you want to use marijuana, you can use it via ingestion by food or pill-form. This chapter will be learning about using hemp seeds as food, ingesting marijuana in an edible form, vaping, joints, bong, hash, oils, and pill-form marijuana. Let's dive right in.

Hemp Seeds as Food

Since hemp is part of the cannabis family, we will be discussing how you can use it as a type of food. Hemp is a plant grown in the northern hemisphere and can be consumed untransformed or used to produce many different food products. These foods include; hemp hearts, hemp milk, hemp cheese substitutes, hemp protein powder, and hemp oil. Hemp seeds have a mild and nutty flavor, while hemp oil has a 'grassy' flavor.

People often confuse hemp with marijuana since it belongs to the same family. However, hemp and marijuana are two very different plants. Let's talk about some of the health benefits that come with consuming hemp. First of all, hemp is a great source of healthy fats. Hemp contains a major source of omega-3, which we normally get from fish. However, hemp is a plant-based source of omega-3, and you can consume it if you don't eat fish or meats.

Hemp is also a great source of protein as it has ten essential amino acids making it a strong source of protein. It also doesn't contain phytates, which we find in most vegetarian/vegan protein sources, which can get in the way of your body absorbing essential minerals. Also, hemp is a great source of magnesium. Magnesium is important as it helps metabolize food, proteins, and acids. Magnesium also plays a huge role in neuromuscular transmission and muscle relaxation. Those who have a magnesium deficiency, likely people at old age, have been linked with osteoporosis, coronary heart disease, metabolic syndrome, and insulin resistance. Hemp is one of the best sources of magnesium out there. Recent research has found that people who suffer from premenstrual syndrome (PMS) may be able to manage/alleviate their symptoms like insomnia, bloating, weight gain, breast tenderness, and swelling by consuming enough magnesium.

You can find hemp products in the form of hemp oil, hemp milk, hemp seeds, and hemp protein powder. Your local health food store or your grocery store's healthy section likely sells all of these foods.

- Other Edibles

Another way to consume marijuana is by eating it in a food form. The 'high' effect that it gives to your body feels much different than the high feeling you get through smoking marijuana. Edibles are all food items that use cannabis concentrates or cannabis flowers as part of their ingredients. In our modern world today, there have been many advances in the world of cannabis culinary, and you are likely now able to find a large selection of high-quality beverages, baked goods, cooking oil, candies, and brownie mixes. You can find the perfect type of food through trial and error to help you ingest THC and CBD to achieve the best high feeling.

The benefits of eating cannabis edibles are the ability to feel the body/mind effects of cannabis without needing to vaporize or smoke the flower. Eating cannabis is simple as everybody knows how to eat or drink, but many people don't know how to smoke or vaporize cannabis properly. However, the disadvantage of consuming cannabis edibles is that your digestive system absorbs them. This action method means that the effects of cannabis can take up to several hours to set in fully and the potency of its effects is very gradual. Depending on the person, the onset of effects may happen as quickly as 15 – 20 minutes or as slow as 3-4 hours. The duration of the effects can last anywhere between 4 to 7 hours.

You can get edibles in nearly any type of form today. Depending on where you live, you may be able to buy products like cannabis, chocolate, butter, gummies, and cookies at your nearest marijuana dispensary. However, if you don't live in an area with legal marijuana edible goods, you may have to make your own through a process of extracting oils from the cannabis flower.

Since your digestive system absorbs edibles, the effects happen in a delayed onset fashion. This onset is much slower than smoking/vaping marijuana. Suppose it is your first time trying marijuana/cannabis. In that case,

I advise that you don't try edibles as it is very easy to take too large of a dose, which will cause strong effects that can lead to puking, paranoia, and insomnia. You can measure the potency of an edible if you are making your own. It is measured differently compared to cannabis flowers or concentrates. Rather than measuring edibles by the percentage of cannabinoids contained within, we measure edibles' potency by the milligrams of cannabinoids within. If you are buying your marijuana edibles from your dispensary, the package should indicate how many milligrams of THC and CBD are within. For instance, if a cannabis brownie had 60 milligrams of THC and your desired dose is 6 milligrams, the brownie can be cut into ten pieces, containing 6 milligrams in each piece.

Depending on your cannabis and marijuana experience level, you want to try edibles slowly and take less rather than more. The recommended edible dose for beginners is anywhere between 1 to 5 milligrams of THC. My recommendation is to start with a dose of 5mg and then wait a full 24 hours to evaluate its effects on you. If you don't feel anything, you can increase your dose by 2.5 – 5mg every 24-hour interval until you feel the desired effects. Once you do feel the effects, that new number will become your minimum effective dose.

I strongly advise you not to take more edibles if you haven't felt the effects in a few hours. Some people may take up to 5 hours to feel the effects of it. If you try to consume more within a 24-hour window, you are putting yourself at risk of taking too much THC/CBD, which may lead to blacking out, vomiting and paranoia. In slang terms, we call this 'greening out.' Although this is generally not harmful, the experience itself is unpleasant and maybe enough to deter you from marijuana forever. Make sure to be safe and smart about consuming edibles and take it from a 24-hour interval to find the perfect balance for your specific body.

- Vaping

Vaping is a more modern way to use marijuana/cannabis. With the recent news on the media, they are shedding more light on new vaping trends. Vaping has always been one of the best and safest ways to consume marijuana. However, with the birth of vape pens that can be nicotine and marijuana, there has been a controversial discussion around this topic. Be warned that there is currently not enough research to confirm or deny how safe vaping is.

Vaporizers or vape pens are the newest and hottest trend in consuming cannabis. To some experts, it is the least harmful method to inhale cannabis. Some scientific studies say that vaporizing cannabis is much healthier than smoking. However, it is safe to say that neither vaping nor smoking something through inhaling is 'healthy' in itself. Still, since vaporizers are a growing trend, there has been a lot of buzz around how people can vape weed most safely and healthily possible.

So how exactly does a vaporizer work? Vapes work by heating plant material and turning it into vapor. Then, the vapor rises, and you then inhale it through a mouthpiece. Not all vapes work the same; there are mainly two types of vapes out there. The more popular one is called the vape pen, which is small and can fit inside your pocket. The second kind is a stationary version that you usually keep at home. Depending on which kind of vaporizer you have, some work by heating the plant material's area. That hot air then surrounds the cannabis, which causes it to released CBD and THC into the air. You can then inhale that through the mouthpiece. The second kind of vapes heats the plant material directly by using a heated surface such as a chamber or a metal plate. Once the plant material is in contact with a hot surface, it releases THC/CBD into the vapor. Once the vapor collects, you can inhale it through the mouthpiece.

Now let's talk a little about how you can vape weed. The first type of vaporizer that you can use is the stationary vaporizer. This type of vape is the more traditional way of vaporizing cannabis and has been around for many years. These machines are quite large and cannot easily move about as a vape pen can. They also require a power outlet to function. Depending on the model, you may need to set it up on the table or the floor, and it will contain a plastic balloon or a small hose. Usually, you use the house to inhale the vapor that comes from the vaporizer. While the balloon gets inflated with vapor, the person using it can inhale from it. To vape, your cannabis/marijuana put the ground weed into the chamber of the vaporizer. Plug the vaporizer into the power outlet to turn it on. Then, select the temperature you want to heat your vaporizer and wait 1 – 2 minutes before inhaling the vapor.

If you are using a vape pen, its usage process is very similar. If you have used an electronic cigarette before (e-cig), you will have no trouble using a vape pen. Charge your vape pen's battery until it is 100%, then fill it up with the desired vaping material. Some vape pens come with THC/CBD oil cartridges, so select the one you want to use and insert it into your vape pen. Next, there should be a button on your vape pen that you can press, which will begin heating the weed/oil. Place your mouth on the mouthpiece and inhale.

Depending on what type of cannabis/marijuana you used to vaporize, you may feel a variety of different highs. Most cannabis strains will give the user a head rush that will make you feel lightheaded. If you begin to feel dizzy, you may likely have vaporized too much. If you are sitting down and feel a 'sinking' feeling, that is another indication of inhaling too much. If you have taken just the right amount, it feels as if the surface you are sitting on is hugging you, and everything feels comfortable and soft.

Remember, depending on which strains you are vaping, you can feel very different types of highs and effects. Some people may begin to think slower and zone out while others may get the giggles. Some strains contain different terpenes which are responsible for different effects. For instance, myrcene is a terpene found in indica cannabis strains and is known for the 'couch lock' type of high feeling. This feeling is when you feel as if your body is locked into whatever surface you are sitting on, and you find no desire to move at all. Some people enjoy this type of sensation while others don't. Finding the right type of strains to vaporize that matches what you're looking for is an important process of properly using marijuana.

In terms of the length of the effects and high through vaporizing marijuana, it varies from person to person. Depending on how high your cannabis tolerance is, it may be longer or shorter. Experienced users may feel anywhere from 30 – 1 hour of 'high' time, while beginner users can feel up to four hours of high. This period is drastically different from edibles, where you can feel the high effects for 5+ hours depending on the person's tolerance and size. This duration is why we do not recommend edibles for beginner users of marijuana. The high takes a long time to fade, causing the person high anxiety to not enjoy it.

- Rolling Joints

Smoking marijuana through a joint is the most common way to inhale marijuana and is the type of method most popularly portrayed through media. This method is convenient for people short on time or does not have the technology, like vaporizers. Vaporizers and edibles can get quite expensive, whereas joints are cheap to make and can give you similar bodily and mental effects. Even with joints, you may have heard of many different types of it; joints, spliffs, and blunts. What exactly is the difference between these three types? Are they just the same thing but have different slang terms to it? The answer to this is that all three of these terms are fairly different. Let's take a look into what a joint, spliff, and blunt are.

A joint has five components: interior, exterior, color, size, and flavor. The inside of a joint is always going to be marijuana; there's nothing else in there. The marijuana can be of any strain you choose. The exterior of a joint is usually some sort of rolling paper or cigarette paper. These papers can be of different materials that can range from wood-pulp to exotic rice and even gold. Different papers differ in size, thickness, flavor, burn length, and 'rollability.' You may recognize some famous rolling paper-like Raw and Zig-Zag brands. When it comes to the color of joints, the traditional colors will always be light-tan or white. However, nowadays, there are unlimited colors for rolling papers ranging from pink to polka dots. The size of rolling papers is approximately three inches long and will resemble a cigarette when fully rolled. The joint can be thicker or thinner, depending on what type of paper you use and how much weed you put inside. Next, the joint's flavor will vary based on the strain you pack inside it, but you can also get flavored rolling papers like a strawberry that will make the joint taste fruity.

Now that we know what a joint is, let's learn about what a blunt is. Just like a joint, the inside of a blunt is 100% marijuana. The major difference between a blunt and a joint is that the blunt exterior uses tobacco paper. You can also use a cleaned-out cigar wrap to make a blunt. Blunts are always colored brown; you won't be able to find any colorful or polka-dotted blunt wraps. When it comes to size, blunts can range heavily. Some blunts can be longer or shorter, and the thickness also changes depending on how much marijuana you put inside. You may come across a blunt that is so fully packed that it looks like a commercial cigar. Less tightly packed blunts look like a drinking straw. All you have to remember is that blunts use either tobacco paper or cigar paper, which makes it a blunt and not a joint. The flavor of the blunt is affected by what type of exterior wrapping you use. The most basic form of a blunt will taste like a mix of marijuana and tobacco. For some, this is a good thing; for others, it is a bad thing. It also takes a lot of experimentation to determine which strain works best mixed with a blunt wrapped of your choice.

Now that you know what a blunt and a joint is, what exactly is a spliff? The main differentiator of a spliff is that the interior of the spliff contains both marijuana and tobacco. Keep in mind that most spliffs normally don't contain more than 50% tobacco; it is still mainly marijuana dominating the interior. The exterior of a spliff is similar to a joint where the rolling paper holds everything together. Due to this, joints and spliffs look almost the same from the outside. It is important to confirm whether you are smoking a joint or a spliff if someone offers it to you. Otherwise, you may be in for a nasty (or pleasant) surprise. Same as joints, the color of your spliff depends on what rolling paper you choose to use. You can use your standard white/tan papers, or you can go crazy and get yourself some gold rolling papers. When it comes to spliff sizes, it depends on what size of rolling paper you are using. Like joints, the average size is 3 inches long, and the thickness is similar to your regular joint. A spliff's flavor will be very different from a joint but may taste similar to a blunt. Keep in mind that a joint is 100% marijuana, so its flavor depends on what strain you use on the interior. Since a spliff is a mix of marijuana and tobacco, the smell and taste may resemble a cigarette more than a joint.

- Bong

Next, let's talk about the bong. The bong is another very common and popular method to consume weed and is probably a stoner favorite. We also sometimes call the bong a *billy*, *binger*, or *bubbler*. Essentially, they are just water pipes used to smoke cannabis or another flower you like. Bongs have been around for hundreds of years, and the name of it came from the Thai word "baung," a bamboo tube that people used to smoke marijuana back in the day. Our modern bongs look much different from the Thai baung, but the science and functionality behind them are still the same.

Your first question must be, how does a bong work? Well, bongs come in millions of shapes and sizes. Most are basic with a chamber and a bowl, whereas other bongs are full-on magnificent art pieces. However, all bongs have the same functionality at the end of the day. What it does is it will filer and cool the smoke that you get from burning your weed. Bongs will have a small bowl that you use to hold your dry marijuana flower. When you light the weed on fire, it combusts and creates smoke. When you inhale the smoke through the bong, the water at the bottom will bubble, the smoke rises through the water and then through the chamber, which will bring the smoke into your lungs.

The main myth around a bong is whether it is better for your lungs than other smoking methods. The bong's water alleviates the dry heat you would normally get if you smoked marijuana through a joint. People commonly describe the effect you get from this type of smoking as the following; smooth, creamy, and cool. However, this effect can be deceptive. Although the smoother and creamier feeling of smoke may feel better on your lungs, you are still smoking something at the end of the day. Smoke is still in your lungs, and that is never good for you. Some of the bad stuff like targets filtered out through the water but not enough of it is filtered out to make a difference if you are a daily smoker truly. So the short answer to this myth is no, bongs are not safer or healthier. Smoking is smoking, and you will compromise the health of your lungs if you do it frequently.

However, there are numerous benefits to using a bong over other methods of smoking. First and foremost, bongs are a great way to smoke marijuana efficiently as it does not get lost. Compared to smoking your weed through a joint or a pipe, the bowl in your bong holds the weed securely until you have completely burnt through it. If you are smoking a joint, a significant amount of weed gets lost in the rolling process or the ashing process. To many stoners, using a bong is the quickest and most efficient way to smoke weed. Another benefit is that you can use your bong inside without having your home smelling like a weed farm. People use a common technique to smoke weed with their bong to open up a window, smoke a bowl, and exhale out their window. You will not be able to do this using a joint or a pipe as the burning process is too difficult to control. Another benefit of using a bong is that you can control exactly how much you smoke. People normally roll joints with differing amounts of weed depending on the papers you use and how steady your hands are that day. A bong, on the other hand, you can measure out how much weed you want to smoke in one sitting and only smoke that much. It is easy to over-consume weed through joints as you can't tell how much you have smoked.

Keep in mind to keep your bong clean and sanitary. Many people make the mistake of never cleaning it, causing a build-up of bacteria that can lead to diseases. There was a case in 2017 where a person developed necrotizing pneumonia due to bong use. This condition is an extremely serious condition that could cause permanent damage to your lungs. Avoid this by changing your water frequently and cleaning it with alcohol often.

- Hash

Hash is a type of extremely concentrated and potent marijuana/cannabis concentrate that you can eat, vape, or smoke. Hash comes from the resinous glands of the female cannabis plant. Hash is gold in color and is sold in almost every dispensary. Hash has a high concentration of terpenes, which are the essential oils that create a more enhanced cannabis effect. Since the hash is extremely potent, I do not recommend that beginners use this kind of marijuana as it is very easy to consume too much of it, which can negatively affect the body and mind.

There are three types of hash out there; traditional hash, bubble hash, and butane hash/solvent hash. Traditional hash has the appearance of dark brown balls with a greasy film on the outside. This kind of hash comes from separating the marijuana flower's trichomes from the rest of the plant by dry sifting it. You then compress these trichomes together to create thick balls. Bubble hash, also known as "ice water hash," is created by washing the trichomes with cold water and then filtering it through a micron bag. Bubble hash varies in its consistency as it could be a fine dry powder or a sticky matter. It can come in different colors ranging from black to light tan. Butane hash or solvent hash comes from using solvents, which help to extract the marijuana compounds. To make this, you expose the flower to a solvent that removes the essential oil from marijuana. You then heat this oil inside a vacuum that evaporates off the solvent used, which leaves you with a highly concentrated hash.

There are many ways that you can consume hash; smoking, dabbing, vaping, and ingestion. Let's take a look at how we can cook with hash. The most effective eating hash method is to reheat it and then blend it into oils and butter that you can use to make edibles. The most popular method is infusing the hash into butter, where you can use it for cooking virtually everything. Hash can be used in recipes to make coffee, baked goods, and chocolate.

The next method is vaping hash. Back in the day, if you wanted to vape your hash, you would have to use the hot knife method. This method happens by placing metal butter knives onto your stovetop. This method can only work on stoves with the metal spiral range top and not the futuristic induction stoves that most people have nowadays. You would place your butter knives on the spiral range top until they got hot. Once the tip of your knife is flowing hot, you will take it off, place a small piece of hash on the knife and press it down with a second knife. This act would vaporize the hash, and you can inhale the vapor that comes from it. You can do this by either just sucking it in with your mouth or using a drinking straw. Luckily, in this day and age, we have come a long way with technology. Vaping hash nowadays is as simple as buying a vaporizer from your local dispensary, which will heat the hash for you into its boiling point, which will create vapor that you can inhale. If you are vaping hash using a vape pen, you want to choose the purest hash as you possibly can. If it is not pure, your hash won't fully melt and leave burnt residue inside your vape pen, causing it to break down much quicker. This method is a less popular method of consuming hash, as many people will opt for a marijuana extract, which is less likely to break down your vape pen over time.

The next method that you can consume hash with is to dab it. Dabbing hash will require you to use a 'dab rig.' A dap rig is a special type of water pipe where you can place your cannabis concentrate onto a hot surface to produce a vapor that you can inhale. Dabbing is similar to vaping, where the hash's cannabinoids can instantly enter your bloodstream to create immediate effects. Same as vaping, the effects you feel from dabbing will differ based on how pure your hash is.

The last method you can use to consume hash is to smoke it. If you are smoking it, you can simply just use the hash itself, but it is difficult to melt, and you may struggle to get a good hit of it without wasting most of it. If you smoke your hash, you can break it into small pieces and mix it into your joint or in the bowl of your bong. When you heat it as you burn it, the hash will turn into oil and create a larger flame. This heat will highly affect how much your joint or bowl burns when you smoke it. This method is the simplest way to consume hash as you don't need much equipment compared to dabbing, vaping, and ingesting.

- Oils

Cannabis Oil is a thick and sticky substance that you can extract from the cannabis plant. It comes from CBD and THC (cannabinoids). At the moment, it is the highest concentrated form of marijuana and has increasingly grown in popularity in recent years. Cannabis oils are great for medical use because it allows the product to have controlled THC/CBD concentrations, making it great for medical use as dosing is easy and accurate.

Cannabis oils that are high in THC give the traditional high that users typically enjoy. However, CBD oil doesn't change a person's mental state, and due to this, it has become an effective and ideal remedy for those who are working or are parents looking for a natural treatment for their ailments. Some reported symptoms include dry mouth, low blood pressure, light-headedness, and drowsiness. CBD oil has been shown to relieve many negative symptoms that can impact a person's wellbeing. These conditions include diabetes, heart disease, insomnia, damaged skin, stress and anxiety, and chronic pain. Specific to CBD oil, it has an antioxidant property that reduces Alzheimer's disease, HIV, dementia, autoimmune diseases, and inflammation.

You can consume cannabis oils using a vape pen or an eyedropper to drop it under your tongue. Both of these methods allow the oil to be ingested and activated very quickly. Those who don't enjoy smoking or want the negative effects of vaping can opt for simply ingesting a dose of CBD oil.

- Pill-Form

You can make THC pills by extracting the THC/CBD within the cannabis plant then is crammed into a gelatin capsule. Although THC pills seem fairly simple, there is still a ton of confusion surrounding it. There are also legal synthetic versions of THC pills out there, but they are by no means the same as natural THC pills. Due to THC pills' amount of information, choosing the right one for yourself can be stressful and scary if you are new to using marijuana.

Marinol is the artificial form of a THC pill, and people who have AIDS or cancer can benefit from this for the relief of nausea and pain. Marinol gives the user a similar high, which has been shown to take effect slower but has longer pain-relieving effects than smoking cannabis.

When it comes to taking THC pills versus smoking it/vaping it, experts argue that taking pills is a more convenient and comfortable option than traditional methods of using it. The major advantage of taking THC pills is that they are significantly more powerful, and its effects last much longer than smoking/vaping marijuana. However, it does take a while for it to take effect similar to edibles, so you must have patience.

Chapter 3:
The Marijuana Plant

Throughout this chapter, we will look at the basics of the cannabis plant in a little more detail than we did in the introduction. We are going to look at the different characteristics that a cannabis plant can have and how to identify them when you begin to grow your own!

Different Strains of Marijuana

When growing marijuana, one very important concept to understand is something called a *strain*. A strain is a type of marijuana characterized by several factors such as the THC content, the type of high that a person will experience, and the appearance of the marijuana plants.

For a novice marijuana user, it may not matter all that much which type of marijuana they choose to use, but as someone who wants to grow their marijuana plants, this will matter much more to you. Also, for frequent marijuana users or those who use it for medicinal purposes, it matters a great deal about which type of marijuana they choose to use. For this reason, it is important for those who are considering growing their marijuana plants to understand the differences that exist between different marijuana strains so that you can provide yourself and your customers with the right product.

Cannabis is a plant that falls into three subspecies or strains; *Indica, Sativa*, and *Hybrid*. We will begin by looking at the first two below, before introducing the third strain later in this chapter.

Indica

The effects of the Indica strain of marijuana include what is known as more of a "body high," which includes relaxation, appetite stimulation, sleep aid, and pain relief. Indicas are recommended for nighttime use as they give the user a sense of heavy relaxation and help to fall asleep. Indicas tend to lower a person's energy and are best for nighttime consumption and is often used to help relax after a full day of work and activities. Strong Indica strains are known to give its users' couch lock', a slang term for feeling so relaxed that the user can barely get up from where they are sitting (usually the couch).

Sativa

The Sativa strain of marijuana plants provides the user with more of what is called a "head high," which includes alertness, euphoric and uplifted feelings, creativity, and increased energy. This strain is best recommended for daytime use as it does not give the same tiredness effects that indicas are known for. Sativas are known to be cerebral and uplifting, helping a person enhance their productivity and even their creativity. While indicas give a person a 'body high' (hence the couch lock), sativas bring more of a 'mind high.'

Similarities and Differences between Indica and Sativa Strains

Indica and Sativa plants are different because they provide the user with very different physiological effects when consumed. They also differ in their outward physical appearance when looking at the plant itself. The main differences between Indicas and Sativas are their medical effects and how they affect the users' productivity levels and energy levels.

Normally, those who use marijuana to treat chronic pain will select an indica as it is known for their pain-killing benefits. However, others who may need to go to work or have family responsibilities may choose sativas as they still require lots of energy to get through their day. When it comes to specific ailments, sativas are much better for psychological disorders such as anxiety, PTSD, and depression. Indicas are chosen more often for disorders like inflammation and pain, helping those with cancer, fibromyalgia, and arthritis. However, since psychological disorders like insomnia and depression accompany so many ailments and diseases, a person must consider choosing a strain that can treat their core disease while managing other symptoms that come with it.

Before marijuana legalization in several countries, the primary way of obtaining marijuana is through the black market. For this reason, indicas were the dominant strain in the black market as it yielded much more and was easier to grow than sativas. However, due to the black market's lack of choice, marijuana users needed to be more careful about what they consumed. They may be in for a nasty surprise if they use a strain that is not compatible with themselves. Luckily in modern-day, professional marijuana growers will breed a wide variety of strains in both indica and Sativa types solely for those who use it to medicate any ailments.

This variety has offered the market a much larger variety of marijuana where one can choose the best strain to match their preference, lifestyle, or disease.

Hybrid

A Sativa and an Indica can be bred and mixed to create a hybrid strain. Indica and Sativa mixes are very common and are known for their 'alert mellowness,' which still allows for productivity.

You make Hybrids by mixing one Sativa with one Indica parent or two Sativa parents or two indica parents. Since there are so many hybrid strains available to us, you can breed many to possess abilities to kill pain while not giving the user a couch lock during the day. Those who use marijuana to medicate during the daytime will often use a Sativa-dominant hybrid that will allow them to function during the day but will switch to an Indica-dominant strain in the evenings for pain relief relaxation. Most hybrid strains available through dispensaries come with a label denoting either 'Sativa-dom' or 'indica-dom.' This is quite self-explanatory as it simply tells you which strain is more dominant. Depending on the dispensary you are purchasing from, strains can be as specific as '60/40' Sativa/Indica or '80/30' Indica/Sativa.

The Importance of Understanding Strains

The method by which you consume marijuana determines how your body processes it and how it leads to your high feeling. When growing your marijuana plants, you will want to have the consumption method in mind, as this could inform which strains you choose to grow.

Over the past few decades, over one thousand different marijuana strains have come to fruition. It is important to understand the different types of marijuana if you use it to treat a certain problem. Some types of marijuana are more appropriate to treat certain ailments and diseases, while others may not have any effect. Choosing the right strain is extremely important when trying to ensure that you can solve your problems with it. However, as I mentioned above, if you are a recreational user that is new to marijuana, strains matter much less to you.

In the modern-day, professional marijuana growers will breed a wide variety of strains in both Indica and Sativa types solely for those who use it to medicate any ailments. This variety has offered the market a much larger marijuana array where one can choose the best strain to match their preference, lifestyle, or disease.

Specific Strains and Their Characteristics

In this subchapter, I will provide you with several examples of specific marijuana strains and what effects they have to offer. This information will help you better determine which strains you'd like to try and what they have to offer, as well as which strains you might like to begin with as you grow your marijuana plants.

Indica Strains

- Blueberry Kush

Blueberry Kush is an A-list cannabis strain that has given itself legendary status. It claimed the High Times' Cannabis Cup 2000 for Best Indica. This strain has a long history dating back to the 1970s, where this strain came about through exotic landrace strains. Throughout the decades of breeding Blueberry Kush, the genetics have changed significantly and produced sweet flavors of blueberries. The taste of this strain, combined with its intense relaxation effects, gives the user a long-lasting euphoria feeling. Many users choose Blueberry Kush to manage their stress and pain, while recreational users admire this strain for its high THC content and colorful hues.

- Granddaddy Purple

Granddaddy Purple or otherwise known as GDP is one of the most famous indicas out there. It's a California staple that is a mix between Purple Urkle and Big Bud. This strain has a complex berry and grape aroma that comes from the Purple Urkle. The oversized bug structure comes from the Big Bud strain. The flowers of Granddaddy Purple is in a shade of deep purple with a snow-like dusting that is white crystal resin. Its effects are potent and give the user both a body and mind high that feels like physical relaxation and euphoria at the same time. Your thoughts may feel as if it's in a dreamy state while your body feels fixed into one spot for the high duration. People normally use GDP to help fight muscle spasms, appetite loss, insomnia, stress, and pain.

- Northern Lights

Northern Lights is one of the most famous strains in the history of marijuana. It is a pure indica known for its resilience during growth, fast flowering, and resinous buds. It is a descendant of the Thai landrace strains and indigenous Afghani strains. Northern Lights has given birth to popular hybrids like Super Silver Haze and Shiva Skunk. Northern Lights is a spicy and sweet aroma that radiates from crystal-coated buds, which is in a purple hue. The effects of Northern Lights' are mainly a body high, which relaxes the users' muscles while relaxing the mind and giving the user a euphoric feeling. This strain offers the user comfortable laziness that effectively relieves pain and sleepiness while its mellow effects help relieve stress and depression.

- Purple Punch

Purple Punch is the product of Granddaddy Purple and Larry OG. It is a sedating and sweet strain that smells like tart Kool-Aid, blueberry muffins, and grape candy. This strain's effects give the user both a head and body high that starts at your forehead and spreads down to your limbs. Purple Punch is a strain that is recommended for usage after dinner as its effects can help with insomnia, body aches, stress, and nausea. Its main effects are feelings of relaxation (73%), happiness (49%), and euphoria (44%). The main drawback of this strain is the 25% likelihood of getting a dry mouth.

- Bubba Kush

Bubba Kush is an indica known for its tranquilizing effects. It is a strain that is very popular in the United States. Its flavors are sweet and hashish with subtle notes of coffee and chocolate that arise when you exhale. Its effects are nearly instant where relaxation takes over during the exhale. Its body high is full encompassing from head to toe, and your muscles feel as if they are light and free. Euphoria will take over the mind. The strain is great at stress relief and uplifting the user's moods. Bubba Kush has a bulky bud structure with colors that range from pale purple to forest green. The only drawback to this strain is that it has a 39% chance of giving the user dry-mouth. However, it is an extremely useful strain in relieving stress.

- God's Gift

God's gift is a strain that has become extremely popular in California in the mid-2000s. Its flavors consist of hash, citrus, and grape. It comes from two strains; OG Kush and Granddaddy Purple. This strain is one that many people love as it gives the user blissful and dreamy effects. This strain is a quick strain to grow as its flowering time only takes about 8 – 9 weeks. This strain is perfect for intense relaxation and gives the user happy and euphoric feelings. There are no real drawbacks at all, just a little bit of dry mouth occasionally.

Sativa Strains

In this subchapter, we will be taking a look at numerous popular Sativa strains. Sativa strains are known for their head-high feelings, creating effects of creativity, energy, and happiness. These strains are best for those who like/need to use marijuana during the day and are best for beginners to dabble with as their effects are slightly less long-lasting and intense.

- Harlequin

Harlequin is a Sativa dominant (75/25) that is known for it's high CBD content. It is rumored to be descended from an Indica in Nepal and is a mix of Thai and Swiss strains. This strain is highly dependable for its alert and clear-headed Sativa effects. The high levels of CBD in this strain make it one of the most effective treatment out there for anxiety and pain. The CBD in this strain helps counteract the THC paranoia that can often arise within un-expecting users. The flavor of this strain is a sweet mango mixed with earthy musk. The main attraction to this strain is the ability it gives its user to relax without feeling sedated and to feel relief without feeling intoxicated.

- Sour Diesel

Sour Diesel is a strain named after its diesel-like smell. It is an invigorating strain known as Sour D. This strain is fast-acting and gives the users a dreamy and energizing high that built the strong reputation it has today. This strain is also great for healing depression, pain, and stress and has long-lasting effects. These effects make Sour Diesel a popular choice for those who medicate with marijuana. This strain first came about back in the 90s, and people say it comes through breeding Super Skunk and Chemdog 91. There aren't many drawbacks that come with this strain besides the occasional dry mouth.

- Tangie

Tangie is another great strain that originated from Amsterdam and has gained international popularity. This strain is similar to the Tangerine Dream, which came about in the 1990s. Tangie is a cross between Skunk and California Orange, which gives itself a strong citrus heritage that is evident in its citrusy and tangerine flavors and aroma. Tangie grows the best outside and produces buds that are sticky but gives relaxed and euphoric effects. This strain is best known for its happiness effects. It gives the user pretty much no negative side effects like a dry mouth at all. Tangie is a strain you should try! Many recreational users love this strain.

- Sour Tangie

Sour Tangie is a mix between Tangie and East Coast Sour Diesel. It is an 80% Sativa that brings the classic aroma of sour Diesel mixed with the elevating and creative buzz that Tangie has. The taste of this strain is strong in citrus, and the structure of this plant is a combination of Tangie and Sour Diesel. Sour Tangie is a fast grower and has a decently quick flowering time that lands somewhere between 9 to 10 weeks. This strain can be grown indoors and outdoors, making it a popular breed for growers to grow.

- Charlotte's Web

Charlotte's Web is a unique Sativa bred in Colorado to have high CBD content but extremely low THC content. This unique feature of the strain is that it helps with many health-related ailments for many people. This strain gained its popularity after being featured on a CNN television show for its effects on a young child named Charlotte, who had a rare seizure disorder. This strain is known for giving the user feelings of relaxation and a strong uplifting feeling. It doesn't have many drawbacks at all and is also well known for relieving pain.

- Island Sweet Skunk

Island Sweet Skunk is a Sativa strain that users enjoy because of its incredible energetic effects. People often describe the flavor as a 'sweet skunk' taste where the tropical fruit flavors will be dominant. The aroma of this strain is fruity and found to be very similar to the taste of grapefruit. This strain originally comes from Canada, where it is a descendant of many other sweet-tasting strains. This plant grows very tall and straight with extremely high-yield. Certain varieties of this plant have a higher CBD content that helps those who suffer from muscle spasms, inflammation, and anxiety. The buds of this strain have orange-yellow hairs.

- Super Silver Haze

Super Silver Haze is one of the most popular and well-known Sativa strains and has won first prize at the Cannabis Cup in 1997 – 1999. This strain comes from a cross between Haze, Northern Lights, and Skunk and is a beautiful Sativa that offers a long-lasting and energetic high. Its uplifting and euphoric effects are great for people suffering from nausea, lack of appetite, and high-stress levels. This strain is commonly found in most dispensaries, as it is a go-to strain that everybody knows and loves.

Hybrid Strains

Now that we've learned numerous Sativa and indica strains, you should begin to have a stronger and deeper understanding of the fundamental differences between Indicas and Sativas. Hybrids can be a combination of both and can feature effects that mimic both indicas and sativas. If you are new to using marijuana, this may be a great place for you to start as you can benefit from the effects of both drastically different marijuana types.

- OG Kush

OG Kush came about in the 90s from Florida, where growers crossed a strain with a Hindu Kush plant and a Northern California strain. This cross resulted in a hybrid strain with a complex aroma made up of spice, skunk, and fuel. This strain brings the user heavy feelings of happiness, relaxation, and euphoria. It helps those who suffer from pain, anxiety, and stress. This strain is so popular that people now use it to create many other strains, such as Headband and GSC. For both beginners and expert marijuana users, this strain is worth a try.

- GSC (Girl Scout Cookies)

GSC used to be known as 'Girl Scout Cookies' and is a hybrid between Durban Poison and OG Kush. This strain's reputation grew so much that it could no longer stay within California's borders and has grown in popularity in many other countries. Its aroma is both earthy and sweet, and this strain will give you an intense sense of euphoria along with full-body relaxation. Just a little bit of this strain will give you a good dose of the effects. This strain has won a ton of Cannabis Cup awards, and patients that require a massive dose of relief find that GSC has amazing appetite loss, nausea, and pain healing properties. GSC is a tall plant with purple leaves and orange-ish hairs. This strain has a fairly longer flowering time- it will take between 9 and 10 weeks to finish flowering fully.

- Gelato

Gelato is a hybrid cannabis strain that comes from Thin Mint GSC and Sunset Sherbet. This strain is from California, and the name originated from its dessert-like and fruit aroma. This trait is a common trait in the

Cookie strain family. The buds in this plant tend to have orange hairs with a dark purple hue. Beginner consumers may want to use this strain with caution as it may be stronger than expected. Expert marijuana users with a high tolerance will love the intense euphoria they will get from this strain. The physical relaxation aspect of this strain hits hard, but many users still find that this strain allows them to be mentally agile enough to remain creative and productive during the day time.

- Pineapple Express

Pineapple Express is an intense strain that is potent and a combination of Hawaiian and Trainwreck. This strain's aroma is similar to mango and apple with a hint of cedar, pine, and pineapple. This Hybrid is hard-hitting with a high that is long-lasting and energetic. This strain is perfect for those who would like a lively and productive afternoon, especially if creativity is necessary. The main effects of this strain are happiness, uplifting, and euphoria. There are pretty much no drawbacks to this strain at all besides the occasional dry mouth. I recommend this strain for both beginners and experts in marijuana.

Depending on your individual preferences, you may prefer Sativa, indica, or a hybrid. If you are a new user,

I would recommend trying out a Sativa first as it provides less intense effects than indicas. Certain indicas are potent, and just a little bit of it will be enough to knock you out.

After reading through this chapter, you now have a solid foundation of knowledge about the possibilities of marijuana. We will build on top of this foundation over the rest of the chapters in this book!

Identifying a Marijuana Plant

Indica and Sativa plants are different in physiological effects and physical appearance.

- Height, Width, and Leaf Size

Sativa plants are taller, skinnier, and appear to be lankier, with pointy and thin leaves. Indica plants are stocky and short with leaves that are chunky and broad.

- Growing Time

Compared with indica plants, Sativa plants require more time to grow and yield fewer flowers. Due to this, indica plants have dominated the market for many years since the sole focus is profit.

- Smell

When it comes to the smell of the different strains, Indica smells skunky, earthy, and musty, whereas the smell of Sativas is spicy, fruity, and sweet. The main difference in the smells of marijuana strains is due to terpenes, which are the molecules within the plant that are similar to cannabinoids.

Compared with indica plants, Sativa plants require more time to grow and yield fewer flowers. Due to this, indica plants have dominated the market for many years since the sole focus is profit.

Male versus Female Marijuana Plants

Marijuana plants are either female or male (known as *dioecious)*. This term denotes a concept that may surprise you, but believe it or not; your cannabis plant will have sex- either male or female. You cannot determine the sex right away, but instead can be seen during the fifth stage of cannabis plant growth- the flowering stage. We will discuss the different stages of cannabis plant growth later on in this book to have a better idea of when to begin looking for this on your plants. At the flowering stage, you will be able to start determining the sex of your plants.

The way male and female plants procreate is similar to how humans will have sex to produce a child. The resulting child will include half of its mother's DNA and half of its father's DNA. Two cannabis plants- one male and one female will come together for reproduction, and the male plant will pollinate the female plant, leading the flowers of the female plant to produce seeds.

If your female plants get pollinated, they will die shortly after that, as it has then achieved its life goal of passing on its genetic material. For this reason, understanding the sex of your cannabis plants is necessary so that you can control the pollination of your plants and the lifespan of your female plant's flowers. You would want to determine the sex of your plant to decide whether or not you want your female plants to get pollinated by your male plants.

If you are looking to attain seeds to sell or re-plant to grow a new harvest, you would want your female plants to get pollinated. If you wish to harvest the flowers or your marijuana plants' buds to sell, smoke, or transform them somehow, you will not want your female plants to get pollinated by the male ones.

How to Tell the Sex of Your Plant

To determine the sex of your plant, you will need to check to see which reproductive organs your plant is showing- male or female. This difference is similar to a human baby, where you must look at their reproductive organs to determine their sex once they have formed. Most people will sell only buds that have not gotten pollinated; therefore, they have no seeds. The buds you can get your hands on- through your dealer or in a store are all produced from female plants, as male plants only pollinate female plants but do not grow buds themselves. Seedless buds are called *Sinsemilla.* You can determine the sex of your plant by looking at the spaces between the nodes of your plant (the area where the plant branches off from the main stem). Similar to male humans, male cannabis plants will have two ball-shaped pollen sacs contained at their nodes. These pollen sacs contain their genetic material, which they would pass on by pollinating a female plant. Female cannabis plants will have something called a *Stigma,* which is a small hair-like structure that is in place to catch the pollen that the male plant produces- this is how they essentially "have sex" and reproduce.

The reproductive organs on a female plant will begin growing somewhere around the fourth week of the plant's growth cycle, but it may take around six weeks instead of some plants. Patience is critical in this stage. When you can begin determining the sex of your plants, their sex organs are not fully developed, so they cannot serve their purpose yet, which gives you time to determine which of your plants are males and remove them before pollination can occur.

Chapter 4:
Growing Marijuana Indoors

This chapter will look at how you can begin to grow a marijuana plant of your own. You now have a solid foundation of knowledge regarding cannabis and marijuana plants, and now we will take it up a notch and look at what it takes to grow marijuana. In this chapter, we will look at the different options available to you regarding growing marijuana plants in your home and what to consider before choosing your method.

Since cannabis is a type of weed, it has incredibly high resilience. Growing marijuana indoors isn't as hard as it may seem. As long as you have a basic knowledge of plants and the ability to follow a set of instructions, this task shouldn't be too difficult for anybody to do. If this is your first garden, you are lucky that you are growing marijuana, as it is a classic "weed" in that it can withstand a wide variety of conditions. If you make mistakes, this plant will be more forgiving than some other plants you could have chosen to grow. The important part about learning to grow cannabis indoors is making sure that you understand the stages of cannabis growth and working with varieties that are easy for beginners to grow.

Since you are reading this book, I assume that you want to grow your marijuana plants indoors, but we will look at a few pros and cons of growing indoor and outdoor if this is something that you are considering for the future.

Options for Growing Marijuana

Typically, there are two methods that growers use to grow their marijuana plants. The first is the traditional method, growing marijuana in soil. The second is a new-age method, which involves something called hydroponics. I will walk you through both methods in this chapter and how they each come with their own set of benefits and drawbacks. I will outline the different options available to you to make the best choice for your marijuana garden.

Growing Marijuana Indoor Versus Outdoor

First, we will learn about some of the differences and similarities between growing marijuana, indoor, and outdoor. If you live in a location with seasons, or if you are considering trying both, this section will tell you all that you need to know when deciding where to grow your marijuana plants.

Cannabis has been grown outdoors for most of its existence since it is a plant that we discovered naturally growing in large fields in various places around the world. It is only in recent times that marijuana has been grown indoors. This change from outdoors to indoors came about mostly out of necessity. This necessity came from the strict laws about marijuana that required growers to keep their cannabis plants out of sight, so they do not get caught growing them. Now that there are more sophisticated ways to grow cannabis indoors, it is a method of choice by many.

The first decision you need to make when beginning to grow a marijuana plant of your own is whether you will grow your marijuana plants inside or outside. There are a few things that you will need to keep in mind to make this decision.

1. Climate

You will need to think about the climate you live in when considering how you will grow your marijuana plant. If you live in a variable climate, and that involves a lot of drastic temperature changes, growing marijuana outdoors will likely prove difficult for you. If you live somewhere consistent in terms of temperature and pre-cipitation, you will have more choice about whether you wish to grow your plants inside or outside.

2. Space Allocation

If you choose to grow marijuana outside, you will be freer to allow your plants to grow freely without wor-rying about the space that they will take up. If you grow your plants indoors, you will need to ensure that you have enough space allocated for your plant to grow, keeping in mind that it could grow quite tall, depending on which particular strain you choose to grow. If you do not have the space to dedicate to your marijuana plant indoors, growing it outdoors will be a better op-tion for you.

3. Control Over The Environment

If you choose to grow your marijuana plant indoors, you will have complete control over every aspect of the environment that your plants are growing in, including the type and amount of light, temperature, water, air, and so on. If you grow outdoors, it is up to the environ-ment in which you live, and the time of year you are growing since this will affect things like the amount of sunlight present, the temperature, and the amount of water the plants are getting through precipitation.

When grown indoors, the marijuana plants that result tend to have higher amounts of THC, as well as a more aesthetically pleasing look. This look makes them great for selling if this is your goal. On the other hand, plants grown outside can receive their light from the sun (instead of from lights trying to emulate the sun), which results in higher yields and stronger plants. This result is assuming that the climate outside is suitable for the growth of marijuana.

Now that you understand some of the factors that you need to consider when deciding whether to grow your cannabis plant indoors or outdoors, we will look at each of these two options in more detail. We will also learn about the options you have within each of these two locations- growing marijuana using soil or using hydroponics.

Pros of Indoor Growing

- You will have complete control of the entire environment and the process (temperature, light, humidity, temperature, oxygen).

- You can better control the outcome of your plants for a more satisfying product
- Some cannabis is better grown indoors, especially if they need very specific conditions to thrive.
- Allows you to grow anytime, anywhere.

Cons of Indoor Growing

- Costs run quite high because you need a lot of equipment
- Contamination can occur and it can be very difficult to get rid of.
- With one pest or disease your entire crop could die
- Lack of natural predators that you would find outside to prevent pests
- You may need to use pesticides indoor
- Takes up space inside of your house

Soil Growing

Growing your cannabis plant in soil is the most traditional medium for growth, both indoors and outdoors. Growing your plant in soil is also the most forgiving method of growth, making it the best choice if you are a beginner grower.

Pretty much any high-quality soil will work for growing cannabis, as long as the soil doesn't have artificially extended realize fertilizer contained within it (such as Miracle-Gro), which is not ideal for growing high-quality cannabis.

Hydroponics

Hydroponics is a method of growing plants that do not require using soil. Instead, a plant's roots are grown in clay pellets, Rockwool, coco peat, water, gravel, or sand. You will mix the nutrients required for the plant in a nutrient solution given to the roots directly. Any water that the plant didn't absorb will be recycled through the system and re-used later.

Many indoor cannabis growers are turning to this new, soilless hydroponic growing method in the modern-day. This method requires the grower to feed the plant with a liquid nutrient solution concentrated with minerals, salt, and nutrients that the plant needs to grow. The plant will absorb these nutrients directly into its roots using the process of osmosis absorption.

Growing your cannabis plant using this method allows for quicker nutrient uptake and can lead to bigger yields and faster growth than traditional soil growth. However, it requires the grower to have higher precision and skill as plants respond quite quickly if they are under or overfed. They are also more susceptible to lockout and nutrient burn. We will discuss these different options later on in this book to learn how to prevent and deal with these different potential struggles.

The History of Hydroponics

The method of hydroponics has many futuristic elements, and you may be surprised to hear that this method has existed for many centuries. Some historians believe that the Hanging Gardens of Babylon back in 600BC began with hydroponic gardens. They concluded that the Aztecs had used hydroponic systems in their farming during the 10th – 11th centuries during their farming ventures on Lake Tenochtitlan.

In our modern-day, hydroponic cultivation has been responsible for some of the best cannabis that has ever been grown. With cannabis cultivation growing in popularity, it has positively impacted nutrient formulation and hydroponic systems. This method continues to help the modern hydroponics method grow. This chapter will teach you about the different hydroponic systems you can use to grow cannabis.

Hydroponics can be defined as a 'loose term' as there are various systems out there that fall under the hydroponic method. The one thing that all hydroponic systems have in common is that the system is always soilless but still can provide your plants with oxygen, nutrients, and water.

Aquaponics

Aquaponics is a method of gardening that does not use soil, similar to hydroponics. Aquaponics is a type of indoor garden that uses the waste produced by fish as nutrients for the system's plants. The fish are an integral part of the system in this case, though this does mean that aquaponics requires a little more work than the other two systems we have learned about so far in this chapter. This type of gardening is good for those who want to keep their garden completely natural, though it can require a lot of work as you are also looking after your fish at the same time as developing your garden.

The difference between hydroponics and aquaponics is that hydroponics relies on chemical nutrients to feed the plants. In contrast, aquaponics uses the waste produced by fish as nutrients for the plants in the system.

This system is created by including fish in the garden system using something called aquaculture. Aquaponics combines aquaculture and hydroponics to create the word aquaponics. This kind of system combines the growth and environment for fish to live and eat while producing waste that will serve the plants included in the system. For this reason, it does not include any soil. If you look at the plants alone, the systems in these two methods are the same, and the only difference is their source of nutrients.

Pros and Cons of Using Hydroponics

Before diving into the details of the different indoor growing options in the next subchapter, we will first examine some of the pros and cons of using hydroponics as a gardening method. The pros and cons will be organized for you below so that you can gain as much information as possible about hydroponics.

Pros of Hydroponics

- Control of Conditions

In a hydroponic system, you have complete control of what goes into it because you have to supply all your garden nutrients. For this reason, you can control what nutrients you want to provide it with and in what proportions, which allows you to take many more factors of your garden into your own hands rather than leaving it in the hands of the outside environment.

- Controlled Environment

Growing in a hydroponics system means growing in a controlled environment. Without the outside world's variabilities and the soil conditions, you have control over many more factors than you would with other methods of gardening. For this reason, hydroponic systems often result in much higher yields than traditional methods.

- Flexibility of Environment

Because this is a controlled system of gardening, you have the freedom to create your hydroponic system anywhere, regardless of what type of environment you live in or what time of year it is. Because you don't need soil at the peak of its condition, you have much more flexibility with this type of gardening than other types. Further, you have the chance to grow your plants all year long if you wish to.

- Less Water Usage

Hydroponic gardening systems use much less water than traditional gardening methods, as in this type of system, you can re-use your water. A hydroponic system is said to use 20 times less water than other traditional gardening systems, so it is much better for the environment in this way.

- Pesticide-Free

Since this type of gardening uses a sterile environment that you can control, you don't need to use pesticides. Pesticides are highly controversial in this day and age, so if you are against using them, this would be a great gardening method for you.

- Takes up Less Space

Hydroponic systems are much more condensed than soil-based gardening to get a high yield with much less space. This benefit is great for those without much space to dedicate to their garden, but who still want as high a yield as possible.

- Requires Less Work

Hydroponic systems require less work than a traditional soil-based garden. This benefit is because soil gardens require you to work on the soil often and in specific ways, such as mulching, cultivating, and so on. In a hydroponic system, this is unnecessary as there is no soil, so it requires much less work overall.

- Faster Growing

Plants were grown in a hydroponic system grow much faster than plants grown in a traditional soil-based manner. We will look at the reasons for this in a later chapter.

- Reliable

Because scientists research hydroponic systems thoroughly, they are reliable because their methods are always tested and perfected. By following the techniques outlined in this book, you can rely on getting a high yield every time!

- Easier to Harvest

When growing plants in a hydroponic system, it is much easier to harvest them there than if you were to harvest your plants out of the soil.

Cons of Hydroponics

We cannot look at the pros without also examining the cons of hydroponics. When determining if this style of gardening is for you, you can examine both the pros and the cons to get a better idea of everything involved with this type of gardening system.

- Supply of Nutrients

Because this type of gardening involves a controlled system, this means that you must be the one to give the plants everything that they need to grow healthily. Without sunlight and soil to feed your plants naturally, you need to supply them with what they need on your own. This maintenance can be time-consuming and difficult for those who are beginners.

- Cost

While there are many pros to hydroponics, the cost is one of the major cons. When compared to traditional soil gardening, hydroponic systems are more expensive. We will look at this in more detail later on in this book, in terms of a cost breakdown, to get an idea of what it will cost you.

- Mistakes Cause Problems

When it comes to gardening in a hydroponic system, there is a chance of making mistakes or of having some things go wrong, just like any type of gardening. The difference with hydroponics systems is that the mistakes can lead to negative effects on the plants much quicker than they would in a soil-based garden. This effect happens because there is no soil in a hydroponic system to buffer any problems and resolve them before they can affect the plants.

- Power Sources Can Be Spotty

If your power source that gives power to your hydroponic system is affected by a power outage or by a spotty power source, this can negatively affect your garden. You must make sure that you are connected to a reliable and constant power source to find success with a hydroponic system.

- Water Quality

As we will look at later on in this book, hydroponic systems need higher quality water than soil-based gardens. High-quality water is required because there is no soil to filter the water. You must have access to good quality water to put into your hydroponic system.

- Plant Diseases

Many diseases affect plants in a hydroponic system that can spread easily through water from one plant to the next. Because water is the growing medium in a hydroponic system, diseases can spread from one plant to the next very quickly, so you must be vigilant when preventing the spread of water diseases. You must keep a close eye on this as the spread could wipe out your entire crop rather quickly.

Similarities and Differences between Soil-Based Gardening and Hydroponics

In this subchapter, we will look at some of the similarities and differences between soil-based gardening and hydroponics. First, the major difference between hydroponics and soil-based gardening is that hydroponic systems grow plants without the use of soil and give the plants chemical nutrients instead of natural nutrients from the soil in which they are grown. Further, hydroponics uses artificial light sources, whereas soil-based gardening most often uses natural sunlight.

In a hydroponic system, the plants can take up water into their roots directly from the water in which they are growing. In soil-based gardening, the plants must wait until water trickles down through the soil to their roots, and thus, less water is available to them. For this reason, hydroponic systems require less water because the water that the plants sit in also acts as a means of feeding them.

When planted in soil, plants will spread their roots as far as possible to get access to as much water as possible. This spreading of roots means that the plants must be grown apart to enable each plant to spread its roots enough. In hydroponic systems, the plants do not need to spread their roots as far because they have unlimited access to water. For this reason, plants can be grown much closer together, which will result in a higher yield per area or a much smaller space needed to grow the same amount of plants.

Another difference between these two methods is that plants get constant access to water, nutrients, and oxygen in hydroponics, which means that they are not reliant on rainfall, sunlight cycles, or fertilizer. For this reason, plants grown in hydroponic systems can grow much faster than those in soil-based gardens as there is much less competition for limited resources.

There is no one method that is better than another, only the right method for you and your purposes. By learning as much as you can about the similarities and differences between different types of gardening systems, you will be able to determine what works best for your personal gardening goals.

How to Choose Your Method of Gardening

You may now be wondering how to choose a method for indoor gardening; soil-based or hydroponics? I understand that you want to make the right choice when choosing a system to grow your plants. If you are looking for a garden that can be grown anytime, anywhere, and that will not require too much space, then hydroponics is a great choice for you. If you are looking for something completely organic that does not require too much attention and you live in an area with good soil conditions and ample sunlight and rainfall, soil-based gardening could be a great choice for you. If you have time to devote and you want something organic, soil-based indoor gardening is for you! If you are looking for something completely organic but does not take up too much space and have time and energy to devote to overseeing it, then an aquaponic system could be great. This option is also great if you wish to grow organic produce or other edible products, as it is organically grown and natural. There is no perfect choice, only the right choice for your specific needs. It is important to note, though, that, in general, a hydroponic system will work best for the widest variety of conditions, environments, and experience levels.

Since you do not need to worry about the hours of sunlight, the average temperature, or any other environmental factors, hydroponics can work for virtually anyone, anywhere, and anytime. The one drawback for some people could be the cost associated with a hydroponic system. Still, as you will see further on in this book, there are many different options and price ranges available to you when choosing a hydroponic system. If you want to grow marijuana all year, regardless of the outside temperatures and sunlight levels, you can do this with a hydroponic system.

Chapter 5: The First Steps for Growing Marijuana

Now that you understand the marijuana plant life cycle and all of the stages involved, we will look at how you can make this happen in your own home! This chapter will look more specifically at the logistics involved when you begin growing your marijuana plant. We will look at what equipment this will require, what you need to do to begin growing your marijuana plants indoors, and other things you should keep in mind when you begin growing your plants.

Throughout this chapter, I will walk you through how to get started with both the soil-based and hydroponics indoor growing methods, but our main focus will be on the hydroponics method, as it is much more involved than the soil-based method.

If you're wondering about the cost and where you can get supplies, don't worry about that, I will teach you all about that too so you can get a good estimate of how much this will cost you and where you can begin to look for supplies.

To make this as easy as possible, I will walk you through the steps of growing cannabis indoors one at a time. Throughout these steps, you will have the ability to branch off and learn about soil growing methods and hydroponics. Let's dive right in.

Steps to Take to Make Your Own Indoor Marijuana Garden

Step #1: Choosing a Cannabis Grow Space

If this is the first time you are growing cannabis indoors, you have to set up the right space to do it. This space doesn't need to be a typical looking grow 'room' like the ones you see in movies. It can simply be a spare room, a cabinet, tent, closet, or the corner of your basement. The most important part is to tailor your equipment and the plants you choose to fit the space. For this reason, choosing the right indoor plant is important as some plants grow too large for a small tent.

For your first project, you ideally want to start with a smaller plant in a smaller place. The smaller your growth is, the less expensive it will be for you to complete your project. It is also way simpler to watch over just a few plants rather than a large amount of them. Also, smaller growth, in the beginning, will be less costly for you if you do end up making mistakes. Keep in mind that many novice cannabis growers will experience obstacles like losing a plant to disease or pests. If you are trying to grow ten plants at once in your first grow, you may end up losing a lot of money if they are unsuccessful, whereas if you started with just 1 – 2 plants, it wouldn't hurt your wallet as much.

However, although we are trying to keep your growth area small, we must also think big simultaneously. When you are designing and creating you grow space, make sure to account for the room that the equipment will need like fans, ducting, lights, and the room that the plants will take up. Cannabis plants can grow to a very large size; in most cases, the plant's size can double or tripe in the early stages of flowering. Be sure that your ceiling is high enough, depending on the strain you decide to grow!

If your grow room is somewhere quite small, like a closet, tent, or cabinet, you can just open the entryway and take out your plants when you are working with them. If this isn't possible, make sure you are accounting for the room you will need to physically use to take care of your plants.

Next, make sure you are maintaining cleanliness. This point is especially important when you are growing your plant indoors. Ensure you are frequently sanitizing your workspace and avoiding growing your plants on raw wood, drapes, or carpeting as these types of spaces are difficult to clean. Another important part of your grow space is to ensure that your light is tightly sealed. If you leak light during dark periods, it can confuse your plant and increase your chances of producing male flowers.

There are a few more things I'd like you to keep in mind when growing cannabis indoors. First, you should ensure that your grow space is placed in a convenient spot as you will need to monitor your plants often and carefully. It is important to check in on your plant every day, and if you are a beginner, you probably would like to check in multiple times in a day until you're sure everything you need to do is complete. If your grow space is in an inconvenient area like in a separate building, it may prevent you from being able to check in on your plant multiple times per day. Secondly, you have to maintain optimal temperature and humidity in your grow space. If your space is humid or warm, you may face more obstacles related to grow-space control. Choosing a dry and cool area with plenty of fresh air is highly recommended. Lastly, make sure you are growing your plant with stealth as you may want to conceal it from potential thieves or nosy neighbors, especially if you are growing cannabis in a country where it isn't legal. Choose a spot where if your fan makes noise, it won't bother others.

Step #2: Choosing Your Grow Lights

Grow light quality in your space is the #1 most important environmental factor that will affect the quantity and quality of your cannabis yield. Choosing the best lighting setup you can afford is the best investment you can make. I will give you a breakdown of the most popular types of grow lights for indoor cannabis plants grows.

- HID Grow Lights

HID stands for high-intensity discharge are the industry-standard lights for cannabis grows. Many people choose HID lights because of their value, efficiency, and output capabilities. They typically cost more than fluorescent and incandescent fixtures, but they can produce a larger amount of light per electricity unit consumed. However, they are less efficient compared to LEDs but often cost 90% less for similar results. There are two main types of HID lamps that you can use to grow cannabis: metal halide (MH) and high-pressure sodium (HPS). MH is generally used during your plant's vegetative state and produces a light that is blue-ish white. The light that HPS produces is more on the orange-red spectrum, and you would use this during the flowering stages of your plant.

The setups for HID lighting require a hood/reflector and ballast for every single light. Certain ballasts are supposed to be used with both HPS and MH lamps, whereas some older models will only run one. If buying both MH and HPS bulbs is not an option for you, start using HPS as they can produce more light per watt. Magnetic ballasts cost much less than digital ballasts, but they are less efficient, run hotter, and are harsher on your bulbs overall. Typically, digital ballasts are usually the recommended option, but they cost significantly more. Beware of purchasing cheap digital ballasts that you may find online because they are not properly shielded. They can cause interference in electromagnetic fields that could negatively affect your radio signals and WiFi.

Unless you plan to grow your cannabis in an open and large area with very good ventilation, you will need to reduce the heat produced by your HID bulbs by buying air-cooled reflector hoods that you can mount. To achieve this, you will require exhaust fans and ducting, which will cost you more money and make it much easier for you to control the temperature in your grow area.

- Fluorescent Grow Lights

Fluorescent light fixtures are very popular with small-scale hobby growers, especially the type that uses high output (HO) T5 bulbs. These are very popular as they cost less money to set up. You can also buy the ballast and reflector in one single package. These lights do not need a cooling system because it doesn't create as much heat as HID does. The main drawback with these lights is that they are significantly less efficient; they generate 20 – 30% less light per watt of electricity. Another factor you have to consider is space as you will require about nineteen four-foot-long T5 HO bulbs to equate the output of one HPS bulb at 600 watts.

- LED Grow Lights

LED (light-emitting diode) technology has been popular for a while. However, only recently has LEDs been used as light fixtures for those who want to grow cannabis indoors. The biggest drawback of choosing LEDs is the high cost. High-quality LEDs typically cost 10x of what an HID could do. However, the benefit of using LED grow lights is that they have a long lifespan, uses less electricity, and creates less heat. The highest quality LEDs out there can generate light on a fuller spectrum, which helps plants produce better quality and bigger yields. Unfortunately, much bad quality LED lights are being sold and produced in the market that companies market towards indoor growers. Be sure to do your research before purchasing LED grow lights; otherwise, you may lose your head-earned money.

- Induction Grow Lights

Induction lamps, or popularly known as electrodeless fluorescent lamps, are a piece of "ancient" technology that recently got adapted to be used by indoor growers. These lights were invented in the 1800s by Nicola Tesla, and these lamps can provide a more efficient and longer-lasting version of the fluorescent bulb. The main downside to these lights is their availability and price.

Step #3: Give Your Plants Air

Plants require a lot of fresh air to thrive, and we all learned in grade school, carbon dioxide (CO_2) is required to complete the photosynthesis process. You will need to have a stable stream of air that can flow throughout your grow room for this. You can easily achieve this by placing an exhaust fan at the top of your grow-area that will help you remove warm air.

Another thing you need to do is to make sure you are maintaining temperatures in the ideal temperature range for cannabis. This temperature range is between 70 – 85 degrees Fahrenheit during the times that your lights are on, and 58 – 70 degrees Fahrenheit when your lights are off. Certain cannabis strains, like indica, are more comfortable in the lower range of temperature while other plants prefer to be grown in higher temperatures.

Choosing your exhaust fan's right size greatly depends on how much heat is being created by your lighting design and the size of your grow area. If you decide to go with HID, your grow space will be very warm, or if you are someone who lives in a region with a warmer climate, you may need to run your lights at night to try to keep the temperatures down. I advise you to set up your lights, turn them on and leave them on for a while. Doing this will help you determine how much airflow is required to keep your grow space at a comfortable cannabis temperature. By doing this, you can properly select an exhaust fan that meets your requirements. If you want to reduce the odor from your cannabis, you can add a charcoal filter onto your fan to help filter out some of the smell. Alternatively, to do this, you can create an artificial sealed environment of your own using a dehumidifier, a supplemental CO_2 system, and an air-conditioner. However, this system is very expensive and is usually not recommended for growing cannabis for the first time. Lastly, a good idea for your grow room is to always ensure a constant light breeze as this will strengthen your plants' stems and help create an environment that is less hospitable for flying pests and mold. You can use a wall-mounted circulating fan for this. Make sure to prevent windburn by not pointing your fans directly at your plants.

Step #4: Pick Your Controls and Monitoring

After choosing which climate control equipment and lights you want to use, you can start to automate their functions. There is expensive and sophisticated equipment available that you can purchase to control CO_2 levels, humidity, temperature, and lights; all a beginner like you will need is an adjustable thermostat switch and a 24-hour timer for your fan.

The timing that you set for your light/dark cycle is extremely important when you are growing a cannabis plant. Ideally, your lights need to be on for 16 – 20 hours over 24 hours during the vegetative growth stage.

You will then need to switch over to 12 hours of light per 24 hours during the time you want them to bloom. You will need to turn your lights on and off at the same time every day; otherwise, you may stress out your plants. Having a timer is essential for indoor growth. You can use your timer for your exhaust fan as well, but it is easier to just spend a couple of extra dollars on a thermostat switch.

Using basic thermostat models, you can easily use your thermostat to set the desired temperature for your grow area and then connect your fan to it. As the temperature begins to rise, your fan will turn on automatically until the temperature falls a few degrees under the threshold. This automation will save electricity and energy and help you maintain a steady temperature in your grow space.

Since you are likely not spending all day in your grow area, using a thermostat with a memory feature will help you when keeping tabs on the environment in your grow space. These devices are small and inexpensive and will show you the humidity level, current temperature, and the readings of the highest/lowest temperatures for the period.

If you'd like to play it safe, I recommended that you get your hands on a pH test kit and keep close by, so you can check the pH of your soil/medium, nutrient solution, and water. The cannabis plant thrives in a pH environment of 6 and 7 in soil and 5.5 – 6.5 in hydroponic media. If your pH rises or falls out of the range, you can cause something that is called 'nutrient lockout.' Nutrient Lockout means that your plants won't effectively absorb the nutrients you are giving it, so ensuring your water and soil are consistently at the right pH levels is important. Ensure you are also testing the nutrient mix you are giving to your plant to make sure it is within this desired range.

Step #5: Choose Your Cannabis Grow Medium

If you are growing your cannabis plant indoors, it means that you have various methods that you can choose from. The method could be the modern hydroponic method or simply a good old fashioned pot with soil in it. Different methods come with their own set of benefits and drawbacks. In this step, we will be looking at two of the most popular methods that growers like to use.

- Soil

Growing your cannabis in soil is the most traditional medium for indoor growth. IT is also the most forgiving, making it the best choice if you are a beginner grower. Pretty much any high-quality soil will work with growing cannabis as long as the soil doesn't have artificially extended realize fertilizer (such as Miracle-Gro), which is not ideal for growing high-quality cannabis.

The best choice for novice growers is to use pre-fertilized organic soil or otherwise known as 'super-soil.' You can use this soil to grow your cannabis plant from beginning to end without needing to add any nutrients. You can even make this yourself by mixing bat guano, worm castings, and other components with high-quality soil and let it sit for a couple of weeks. Or, you can just purchase it pre-made from different suppliers.

When it comes to growing your plants organically, this method's fundamentals require you to have the right amount of soil bacteria and mycorrhizae to facilitate the conversion of organic matter into nutrients that your plant can consume. Alternatively, you can purchase a regular soil mix and provide your plants with liquid nutrients when your soil has depleted.

- Soilless (hydroponics)

In the modern-day, indoor cannabis growers are turning to soilless hydroponic media at a fast rate. This method requires the grower to feed the plant with a concentrated solution with minerals, salt, and nutrients the plant can absorb directly using the roots through the osmosis process. This technique allows for quicker nutrient uptake and leads to bigger yields and faster growth. However, it requires the grower to have higher precision as plants will quickly change if they are under or overfed. They are also more susceptible to lockout and nutrient burn.

This method can utilize different materials like coco coir, perlite, expanded clay pebbles, vermiculite, and Rockwool. Commercial soilless mixes are widely available for purchase, and if you take two or more of these media and combine it, you can create an optimized growing mix of your own. You can also automate this, just like soil media in a hydroponic set up or individual containers that require manual watering.

Step #6: Determine What Medium to Grow Your Cannabis In

Choosing the container that you will grow your cannabis in will highly depend on your plant's size, the system, and the medium. For instance, a flood-and-drain, the tray-style hydroponic system may utilize small net pots filled with clay pebbles or even just a big slab of Rockwool to grow several little plans. Consequently, a 'super-soil' grow may use 10-gallon nursery pots to grow a few large-sized plants.

If you are looking for the least expensive option, you can choose between cloth bags or perforated disposable plastic ones. Some people may decide to purchase 'smart pots' and spend a little money. Smart pots are containers designed to better the airflow for your plant roots. The most common medium for first-time growers is simple five-gallon buckets. The key here is drainage. Since cannabis plants are sensitive to water-logged conditions, you must be sure to drill holes at the bottom of the container and set them in trays to allow excess water to leave the medium.

Step #7: Feed Your Cannabis Plants Nutrients

To grow a cannabis plant of high-quality, you will require more nutrients and fertilizers compared to other common plants. Your cannabis plant requires these following macronutrients: Nitrogen (N), Phosphorus (P), and Potassium (K). You will also need these following micronutrients but in smaller quantities: Copper, Calcium, Iron, and Magnesium.

If you chose not to use a pre-fertilized organic soil mix, you might need to feed your plants at least once a week using a good nutrient solution. You can find these sold at garden stores in a concentrated powder or liquid form meant for simply mixing with water. Cannabis has to change macronutrient requirements throughout its entire lifecycle. For instance, it needs more nitrogen during the plant's vegetative stage and more potassium and phosphorus in its bud production stages.

Usually, macronutrients sold in stores are sold in two-parts to help the elements from precipitating, causing waste. Using this style of nutrients means that you will need to purchase two bottles for its vegetative state and two bottles for its grow state and a bottle of micronutrients. Besides that, there is a possibility that you may need to purchase a Cal/Mag supplement because certain strains of cannabis will need more magnesium and calcium compared to other strains.

When you have chosen your nutrient product, all you have to do is combine them with water as per the label instructions. Then, water./feed your cannabis with that solution. Always start watering your cannabis with half-strength because cannabis plants are easily burner. In most cases, it is overfeeding your plants is worse than underfeeding them. Once you have gained more experience with feeding your plants, you will slowly learn how to 'read' your plants for signs of excess or deficiencies.

Step #8: Water Your Cannabis Plants

A lot of people don't think about the water that they use to water their plants. They assume that if you can drink that water, then it should be fine, right? Depending on where you live, this may not be an issue, but certain locations in the world have water that has a high density of minerals and could cause a build-up in the roots of your cannabis plant and negatively affect your plant's nutrient uptake. Or, it could even contain pathogens or fungus that may not hurt humans but could lead to diseases (like root disease) in your cannabis plant.

Moreover, there are some places in the world where the water supply has high levels of chlorine. Chlorine is harmful to certain soil microbes that are beneficial to plants. Due to this, many people decide to take the extra step to filter the water they use for their plants.

One crucial thing to remember during this phase of your cannabis growth is never over water. Like I mentioned earlier, when conditions are too wet, cannabis plants can be susceptible to fungal root diseases. Novice growers commonly make the mistake of overwatering their cannabis plant. The frequency of your cannabis plant waterings depends on the plants' temperature, size, and what medium you decide to use. Some people like to wait until the lower leaves of your cannabis plant begin to droop before watering it. When you gain experience and knowledge throughout this book and your hands-on experience, you can better alter your grow room and equipment to fit the particular needs of your plant and space.

Different Types of Hydroponic Systems

In our modern-day, hydroponic cultivation has been responsible for some of the best cannabis that has ever been grown. With cannabis cultivation growing in popularity, it has positively impacted nutrient formulation and the development of effective hydroponic systems. This method continues to help the modern hydroponics method grow. In this section, I will lay out all of the different hydroponic systems you can use to grow cannabis. Once you understand them all, you can choose the best one for your purposes, depending on your intended use for the marijuana and the amount of space and money you have.

Deep Water Culture (DWC)

Deepwater Culture (DWC) is the simplest form of all hydroponic systems. DWC is a system that is easy for beginners to learn, as it is simple to run and cost-effective. The idea behind this is simple. Start with putting your plants in individual containers and place each of them in a grow tray. Then put your grow tray inside so that it sits suspended in water. If you don't want to do this, you can buy a DWC hydroponic kit to give you customized pots to hold water individually.

In the DWC system, the water tank will utilize an air pump to pump oxygen into the water, and the nutrients are fed to your plants by adding it directly into the water so the plants can absorb it using its roots. Plant roots can remain 100% underwater and still get oxygen due to the air pumps.

Nutrient Film Technique (NFT)

Different from the super simply DWC system, the NFT technique is more complicated. In this system, you have to take the water, oxygen, and nutrient solution and pump it into your planting tube from your reservoir. Expert growers will utilize PVC tubing to drain the water solution down the planting tube by placing the tubing at an angle of small decline, which allows it to pass by all plant roots before it is recycled back into its holding tank.

A common issue with this system is that the water may not effectively drain from the tube. If water sits stagnant for too long, bacteria can grow very quickly and cause your plants to get mold, diseases, or pests, which can lead to death. You can prevent this issue by angling your planting tube at a steep enough decline so your water solution can drain through 100%. Bear in mind that root density plays a role in clogging the chamber as they can grow thick and fast when thriving in ideal environments.

A benefit to the NFT system is that it can expand easily. You can simply just add extra holes in your tube to increase the number of plants that it can hold. Alternatively, you can add extra tubes, allowing you to grow more plants as long as your holding tank and pump can handle the extra plants.

Ebb and Flow

Different from the DWC and NFT system, the E&F system will not submerge your plant roots in water the entire time. It is similar to an ocean tide where it will come in and out of mangroves. This system allows the tray to fill up with the oxygen/nutrient water and will feed the plants when full. Then, the pump will turn off, which will allow the oxygen/nutrient water to drain back into your reservoir, where it will remain until your plants are ready to be fed/watered again. Once it is full, the pump will switch off, and the solution will drain back down into the reservoir where it will stay until your plants are ready to be flooded again. This cycle repeats itself at your desired intervals.

This technique is a great system for growers to use as the roots can take in large amounts of oxygen when the tray is not flooded. It will allow you to harvest your plants quickly and allows you to easily add more plants or take away some plants if you wish.

Drip System

We learned about the drip system briefly in the previous chapter, as it is the most popular system for growing cannabis. In this system, you use individual drippers strategically placed inside each of your plant's growing medium. This way, you can provide your plant with the right amount of nutrient/oxygen water for every individual plant. Any solution that wasn't used by your plants will then be drained back into your reservoir, where you can use that same solution to be pumped back through the dripper system to get used again.

The perks of using this system are that it allows you to harvest and swap your plants quickly by taking away the dripper in your medium. If you are using a dripper system with customizable flows, you can easily control the amount of your solution each plant is getting. On top of that, you can control the watering schedule and choose your plants' frequency of watering.

Aeroponics

Aeroponics is probably the most unique type of hydroponic system out there. In this system, the nutrient/oxygenated water solution will be taken from the reservoir and then pumped through misting valves that spray a fine mist into chambers containing the exposed plant roots. By growing your plants aeroponically, you give your plants the maximum amount of oxygen possible without continually soaking its roots in water. However, aeroponic systems are costly to set up. Still, they are extremely effective if you are growing plants on a commercial scale because they allow you to grow vertically, which maximizes growth space. The biggest concern for this system is clogged misting valves. If this happens and you don't notice, your plants will quickly die if they do not have moisture in the roots.

Wick System

The wick system is probably the most basic hydroponic system alongside with DWC. Like DWC, this system uses a rope, or similar material pulled through a PVC tube. An oxygenated water solution is then pulled up this rope/material and dispersed/released into a growing tray. If you use this method, you don't need a water pump to bring your oxygenated/nutrient solution to your plants, which means less cost and one less piece of equipment that could break down. This system is a super simple system that you can use to properly understand hydroponics before investing in more complicated setups.

Hydroponic Growing Mediums

The list of hydroponic growing mediums that one could use is virtually infinite, but we will learn about the three of the most efficient and common ones. Different types of mediums vary in their ability to retain water and allow oxygen. You can use them in various ways to contain and support plants. As you gain more experience with hydroponics, you will discover which mediums best suit your plants and systems.

Rockwool

Rockwool comes from thin rock fibers created by heating rocks to a very high temperature and then spinning them to create small threads. For cannabis growers, Rockwool has been a favorite due to its strong ability to retain moisture and the ability to breathe. When you are using Rockwool, you need to soak it in a pH solution before using it. Doing this is simple, prepare a pH solution with a reading of 5.5 and then soak your Rockwool in that solution between 8 – 12 hours. Once that is complete, re-check your pH solution reading. If it comes up as between 5.5 – 6, then your Rockwool is ready to be used.

Clay Pellets

Another common medium that is also reusable is clay pellets. Clay pellets are heavy enough to support and hold down your plants and light enough for you to work with simply. This medium can wick up moisture towards the roots while allowing for plentiful of oxygen to flow through.

Coconut Fiber

Like Rockwool but more sustainable, coconut fibers used to be a waste product that people have now discovered is a wonderful growing medium for hydroponics. Coconut fibers allow more oxygen to flow in and retain more moisture than Rockwool, which led to its popularity. Also, coconut fibers have plant-stimulating hormones that will protect your plants' roots from disease and infection.

What You Need to Grow Marijuana Using Soil

In this section, we will look at what you will need to grow cannabis in soil. One of the positives of growing your marijuana plant in this way is that you do not require too much equipment, as this is how marijuana originally go discovered while growing without any human intervention. Below are the different items needed to grow marijuana outdoors in soil.

- Fertilizers And Soil

Soil, at its core, is a combination of earth, organic materials, and some clay and some rock. Soil naturally contains elements that contribute to plant growth, which is why you find plants growing naturally in the wild with no help from humans.

When it comes to choosing your soil mixture, there are a few things that you should keep in mind. For most regular plants, we can find them growing in one of three common soil types. These soil types are below.

- Sandy soil
- Slit soil
- Clay soil

When it comes to growing cannabis, in particular, it requires a certain soil type to grow and thrive. This soil type is a mixture of the three common soil types seen above. This soil type is called *Loam Soil.* The texture of loam soil is somewhere between sand and clay, so it will compact but not hold its shape too well once compacted.

To choose your soil from a store, you can purchase any high-quality soil, but you must make sure that the soil you choose doesn't have any "artificial extended-release fertilizer" contained within it (such as Miracle-Gro). This type of soil is not ideal for growing high-quality cannabis because it does not contain the proper nutrients for growing a great cannabis plant. If you are new to growing cannabis, your best soil option will be a pre-fertilized organic soil. This pre-fertilized soil is often called 'super-soil.' You can use this soil to grow your cannabis plant from beginning to end without needing to add any nutrients. For this reason, it is a great choice for beginners, who will already have several things on their mind when growing their first cannabis plant. You can purchase super soil in a pre-made form from several different suppliers, or you can opt to make your own if you have a little more experience.

If you want to make your own super soil mix, you will need to get your hands on the following ingredients (or some accessible form of these ingredients).

1. A regular potting mix

This mix will act as the base for your soil

2. Vermicompost

This mix is a mixture made of worm casings that is great for your soil's natural nutrients to help your plant grow.

3. Sources of Nitrogen, Magnesium, Potassium, and Phosphorus

These elements can come from various sources, so check your local gardening stores and see what is available in your area.

Once you have added your ingredients together, let it sit for a couple of weeks, and it will be ready to help you grow healthy cannabis plants.

- Water

You will need a water source such as a hose or a spray container to ensure that your plants are getting adequate hydration.

- Marijuana seeds

You will need to get your hands on some seeds or some cloned marijuana plants to begin your plant growth.

What You Need to Grow Marijuana Using Hydroponics

Let's take a look at all the equipment and supplies you will need to run your own hydroponics system. There are numerous different types of hydroponic setups, all with their own unique costs associated. I will walk you through what a standard hydroponic system requires, and I will include the costs associated with this to get an idea of what this will cost you, to help you decide what kind of system you will be using to grow your plants.

- Exhaust Fan

Plants require a lot of fresh air to thrive, and we all learned in grade school, carbon dioxide (CO_2) is required to complete the photosynthesis process. Creating this environment will require you to have a stable stream of air that can flow throughout your grow room. You can easily achieve this by placing an exhaust fan at the top of your grow-area that will help you remove warm air. Choosing your exhaust fan's right size greatly depends on how much heat is being created by your lighting design and the size of your grow area.

If you live in a region with a warmer climate, you may need to run your lights at night to try to keep the temperatures down. I advise you to set up your lights, turn them on and leave them on for a while. This sort of test will help you determine how much airflow is required to keep your grow space at a comfortable temperature for your specific plants. By doing this, you can properly select an exhaust fan that meets your requirements.

- Dehumidifier

As an alternative to an exhaust fan, you could use a dehumidifier. You can create your artificial sealed environment using a dehumidifier, a supplemental CO_2 system, and an air-conditioner to keep the moisture and the heat levels down. However, this system is very expensive and is usually not recommended for first time hydroponics growers before they have had at least a few successful yields first.

- Thermostat Controls

After choosing which climate control equipment and lights you want to use, you can start to automate their functions. There is expensive and sophisticated equipment available that you can purchase to control CO_2

levels, humidity, temperature, and lights, but for a beginner, this may not be necessary. All a beginner like you will need is an adjustable thermostat switch and a 24-hour timer for your fan. Using basic thermostat models, you can easily use your thermostat to set the desired temperature for your grow area and then connect your fan to it. As the temperature begins to rise, your fan will turn on automatically until the temperature falls a few degrees under the threshold. This automation will save electricity and energy and help you maintain a steady temperature in your grow space. Since you are likely not spending all day in your grow area, using a thermostat with a memory feature will help you when keeping tabs on the environment in your grow space. These devices are small and inexpensive and will show you the humidity level, current temperature, and the readings of the highest/lowest temperatures for the period that you set.

- pH Test Kit

I strongly recommend that you get a pH test kit and keep it handy, so you can check the pH of your growing medium, your nutrient solution, and your water. Depending on your plant, it will thrive in certain pH ranges, and you want to ensure that you are maintaining this. If your pH rises or falls out of the range, you can cause something that is called 'nutrient lockout.' Nutrient Lockout means that your plants won't absorb the nutrients you are giving it, so ensuring your water and soil are consistently at the right pH levels is important. Ensure you are also testing the nutrient mix you are giving to your plant to make sure it is within this desired range.

- Growing container

Choosing the container that you will grow your plant in will depend on the size of your plant, the hydroponic system you have chosen to use, and the growing medium you will be using.

For instance, if you are using a flood-and-drain system. This tray-style hydroponic system may utilize small net pots that are filled with clay pebbles or even just a big slab of Rockwool to grow several little plants. On the other hand, a 'super-soil' growing system may use various 10-gallon nursery pots to grow a few large-sized plants. If you are looking for the least expensive option, you can choose between cloth bags or perforated disposable plastic bags.

Some people may decide to purchase 'smart pots' and spend a little more money on them. Smart pots are containers designed to better the airflow for your plant roots. The most common medium for first-time growers is the simple five-gallon bucket. The key here is drainage. Since plants are sensitive to conditions that contain too much water, as they can become waterlogged, you must be sure to drill holes at the bottom of the bucket and set the bucket on a tray to allow excess water to leave the medium to avoid this problem.

- Nutrients

Your plant will require you to add nutrients to it as there is no soil involved. Your plant will require the following macronutrients: Nitrogen (N), Phosphorus (P), and Potassium (K). You will also need these following micronutrients but in smaller quantities: Copper, Calcium, Iron, and Magnesium. Usually, macronutrients sold in stores are sold in two-parts to help the elements from precipitating out of the solution, as this would cause waste. This process means that you will need to purchase two bottles of nutrients for the plant's vegetative state and two bottles of nutrients for its growth stage as well as a bottle of micronutrients. Besides that, there is a possibility that you may need to purchase a Cal/Mag supplement because some specific plants will need more magnesium and calcium when compared to other plants. This part will depend on the specific plant that you are growing.

When you have chosen your nutrient products, all you have to do is combine them with water as per the label instructions. Then, water your plants with that nutrient solution to feed them. Always start watering your plants with a half-strength solution because some varieties of plants get easily burned if they receive too many nutrients too quickly. In most cases, overfeeding your plants is worse than underfeeding them. Once you have gained more experience with feeding your plants, you will slowly learn how to 'read' your plants for signs of excess nutrients or nutrient deficiencies.

The Cost of Growing Marijuana Indoors

The total cost estimation for running your hydroponics system for your first growth will be approximately $730. You can see the breakdown of this cost below. Bear in mind that you can opt for less expensive equipment like choosing cheaper lights like CFL compared to LED. You can also choose to buy a prepackaged hydroponics starter grow kit that may be slightly easier and cheaper for you to use that costs about $500. It typically comes with a 2' x 2' grow tent, nutrients, digital timer, pH drops, adjustable hangers, lighting, CO2 bags, and a clip fan. Keep in mind that electricity also costs money, depending on where you live. Although this cost isn't very high, you will notice an increase in electricity consumption when you start to grow plants indoors. More sophisticated grow kits are on the market, starting from $1000 that you can purchase. Decide what is best for you and go with it! Make sure you are doing your research and look out for sales and promotions when doing this.

Hydroponics Equipment Cost Breakdown

- 3- or 5-gallon bucket, you will need one for each plant you grow ($20+)
- Clay pellets (enough to fill the bucket) ($30+)
- Grow table ($75 - $150+)
- Rockwool cubes (one 1.5inch starter plug per plant) ($10+)
- Water pump (as big as possible) ($20 - $50+)
- Reservoir tank (depends on the size of your garden) ($25+)
- Airstone ($6+)
- Air pump ($12+)

- Plastic tubing ($5+)
- Dripline ($15+)
- Dripline emitters (1 – 2 per plant) ($12+)

Other Equipment:

- Cannabis seeds (feminized seeds) ($10+)
- Grow tent (2' x 2' or 3' x 3') ($120+)
- Nutrients ($50+)
- Lighting equipment of your choice:
    - HID ($200+)
    - LED ($200+)
    - CFL ($50+)
- Carbon filter ($100+)
- pH testing kit ($20+)

The total cost estimation for running your hydroponics system for *one* cannabis plant is approximately $730

Bear in mind that you can opt for less expensive equipment like choosing cheaper lights like CFL compared to LED. You can also choose to buy a prepackaged hydroponics starter grow kit that may be slightly easier and cheaper for you to use that costs about $500. It typically comes with a 2' x 2' grow tent, nutrients, digital timer, pH drops, adjustable hangers, lighting, CO_2 bags, and a clip fan. Keep in mind that electricity also costs money, depending on where you live. Although this cost isn't very high, you will notice an increase in electricity consumption when you start to grow cannabis. More sophisticated grow kits are on the market, starting from $1000 that you can purchase. Decide what is best for you and go with it! Make sure you are doing your research and look out for sales and promotions when doing this.

Chapter 6: The Marijuana Plant Growing Stages

In this chapter, we are going to learn about the cannabis plant itself. The cannabis plant is a plant that requires certain things for it to grow and bloom into beautiful flowers that can then bring you pleasure and happiness in the form of CBD and THC. We will look at the stages that a marijuana plant goes through and how you can grow the healthiest possible marijuana plant by choosing the right amounts of water, sunlight, and food for your plants. This chapter will help you learn how to get the most of your marijuana seeds for whatever your purposes may be.

There are a few things to know about cannabis plants before we begin this chapter. The first thing is that cannabis plants can be either male or female. The second thing is that growing a cannabis plant will take somewhere between four and eight months. You must be patient when growing a plant as it takes time and cares to get it right.

Stage 1: The Seed Stage

The first stage in the cannabis plant life cycle is the seed. This stage is what you begin with before you plant anything and before anything has grown. There are a variety of ways that you can get seeds to plant to grow a cannabis plant.

The seeds of a cannabis plant come from another cannabis plant. These seeds are the plant's way of passing on its genetic material to make progeny plants. The seeds contain information about the mother and the father of the plant, just like humans. Marijuana plants are either female or male (known as *dioecious)*. This genetic makeup is similar to how humans will have sex to produce a child. The resulting child will comprise half of its mother's DNA and half of its father's DNA. This process is the same for a plant. Two cannabis plants-one male and one female, will come together for reproduction, and the male plant will pollinate the female plant, leading the flowers of the female plant to produce seeds.

After a male plant pollinates the flower of the female plant, the female plant will start dying, as it has then achieved its life goal of passing on its genetic material. When this happens, one of two things will happen to the female's seeds.

1. They will fall to the ground and begin the next stage of the plant life cycle, leading to the growth of a new plant made from the original female and male plants.
2. Farmers will harvest the seeds, and he or someone else will turn them into oils, food products, or sold as seeds for others to plant. The farmer may also plant the seeds in their desired locations to harvest later.

When you get your hands on marijuana seeds, you can determine their quality by the look and feel. They should be brown in color, a light or a dark brown. They should also be dry and hard to the touch. Your seed must be mature enough to grow into a plant. If the seeds are white or green in color and soft to the touch, they will not grow into a plant as they have not adequately matured.

Once you plant the seed, it requires some attention to bring it to life. It is not ready to begin growing until it receives some attention. What it needs at this stage is water. We will get into this in the next stage, becoming important for reaching the next stage of the cannabis plant life cycle. Before you begin to germinate your seeds, make sure that you have allowed enough time and space to care for your plant and allow it to grow freely. Doing this will help promote its success.

Stage 2: Germination

The next stage of the cannabis life cycle is called Germination. This stage involves the first stages of change in the seed, and it begins the growth of your plant. This stage will take somewhere between five and ten days. Some people refer to this stage as "the popping stage" as it involves the "popping." As I mentioned, this stage is encouraged by watering the planted seed. They also require heat and air. These three components are what will lead your plant to pop in just the right way. I will outline one of the most common methods for achieving cannabis seed germination below so that you can follow along and try it for yourself.

To begin germinating your seeds, you will need to have access to paper towels and distilled water. Begin with three to five pieces of paper towel and put them together in some distilled water enough to soak. When you remove them from the water, let the excess water drip off them and don't proceed to the next step until they have finished dripping and are soaked but not spilling over with water. Take two soaked paper towels and put them down on a surface like a plate or a dish.

Take your cannabis seeds and place them on top of the soaked paper towel, leaving enough room between each seed- about an inch or so. Put the rest of your paper towel pieces on top of your seeds on the dish, so they remain sandwiched between two layers of paper towel. Take another plate, dish, or bowl and flip it upside-down on top of the seeds covered with paper towels soaked in distilled water. This setup creates a moist, dark, and warm space where the seeds can comfortably begin to germinate. Keep this contraption somewhere warm enough for the seeds to stay humid (preferably between 69- and 89-degrees Fahrenheit).

After you have done these steps, you must wait for your seeds to germinate. You can occasionally check to ensure that the paper towels are still moist enough while you do this. If they are beginning to dry out, saturate them again with water to maintain an ideal germinating environment.

You will know that your seeds have reached germination when they have "popped" or split open, and you can see a small sprout that has begun to grow from this split area of the seed. The amount of time this takes will depend on the seed, so be patient with your little seeds. One important thing to note is that when your seed splits and you start to see the sprout, it is important to keep this area free of contamination. One of the most common contaminants is human hands. Keep your hands away from the sprout as it is the part of the plant that will become the main stem, and you must refrain from interfering with it. This part of the germinated seed is called the *Taproot.*

Once your seeds have germinated, you are ready to plant them in soil. This part is when you are ready to begin growing your plant. Begin with a small pot and some lightly packed soil. Using a small cylindrical device like a pen, poke a hole in the soil. This hole will be where you insert your seed. To avoid contaminating your Taproot, pick up your seed using chopsticks or tweezers and transfer your popped seed into the small pot of soil. When you place it into the soil, ensure that the Taproot is facing down, which may be counter-intuitive, but it is the correct way to plant your germinated seed. When you put it into the hole, push it down into the soil about one-quarter of an inch. Cover the exposed seed or the top of the hole with some soil.

Once you have planted your germinated seed, you will need to begin watering it. You can do this using a small spray bottle so that you do not over-water your plant. You will need to provide the seed with just enough water to grow, but not so much that the seed cannot get any air. Growing a plant is a delicate balance. You also need to ensure that your seed stays warm enough. Keep it in a warm environment, away from any windows if you live in a cold environment. Choose somewhere warm, water the seed lightly, and the darkness factor is already taken care of for you. Your seedling will begin to show through the soil in about a week if everything goes as planned.

You must remember that when waiting for your seed to sprout, there are many factors at play. This part requires patience and an understanding that seeds are very delicate. Further, every seed is different, and you must remember that not all seeds will respond or behave in the same ways. Some may take longer to sprout than others, and some may not sprout at all. Some seeds cannot sprout for one reason and another, so planting many seeds at once is the best option. If some have sprouted but not others, they may take a bit of extra time and attention.

As your plant begins to grow out through the soil, you will begin to see two small leaves form on the stem. These initial leaves are a great sign, as they will capture sunlight and use it for the plant's nutrients and health. At this stage, the plant will grow out of the seed's casing and grow independently. The plant roots will be growing beneath the soil, spreading out to anchor the plant in the soil in preparation for it to grow bigger and bigger. Once you see the first set of "weed leaves" growing on the stem of your plant (those leaves that are internationally known to symbolize marijuana), then this is when you can begin calling your plant a seedling. This step brings us to our next stage in the cannabis plant life cycle, the Seedling Growth stage.

Stage 3: The Seedling Stage

This stage of the cannabis plant life cycle can take anywhere from two to three weeks, depending on the seedlings. The first classic "weed leaves" that you see growing will only have one leaf per set, instead of the traditional 5 or 7 leaf sets used to see on cannabis plants. As more leaves grow, you will begin to see the leaves becoming more and more like those traditional marijuana leaves as the plant matures. The classic marijuana leaves will have somewhere around five and seven leaves on each set. Your plant should have bright green leaves in color; this is what indicates a healthy and thriving plant.

One very important thing to keep in mind is that you must not over-water your seedling at this stage. Underneath the surface of the soil, the roots are still young and have not fully developed yet. They still need air, and giving them too much water can lead them to suffocation as they will not have enough room for air in this case. A small amount of water regularly will be enough to keep your seedling healthy and vibrant. It is also important not to over-water your plant at this stage because it is very susceptible to mold. Having excess moisture in the soil and around the plant can lead it to develop mold. In this susceptible stage, it can easily catch several plant diseases, which can compromise the further growth and prosperity of your plant, not to mention the level of confidence you can have when ingesting the resulting flowers.

Your plant will be a seedling until it begins to grow leaves with the traditional number of leaves per set. When each new set of leaves grows, it contains the number of leaves per set, which has progressed to the next stage.

Stage 4: The Vegetative Stage

Once your plant is no longer considered a seedling (when it begins to grow traditional marijuana leaves with 5-7 leaves per set), it moves onto the next stage called the Vegetative stage. This stage can vary greatly in length, lasting anywhere from three to sixteen weeks in length. The amount of time this stage lasts can depend on several factors, which we will examine here.

The plant will begin to grow much bigger and faster during the Vegetative state than it has yet. When your plant has reached this stage, you will be ready to transfer it into a bigger pot. Transferring it into a bigger pot will allow it to grow freely and without restriction. The roots will begin to grow and mature quickly as well as the leaves.

Training and Topping In the Vegetative Stage

At this stage, you can begin doing two things to your plant; *Training* it and *Topping* it. We will look at what these two terms mean here. Training your plant is done to maximize your possible yield and the buds' potency that your plants create. The practice of training your plant involves intentionally changing the chemical balances by interfering with the plant's growth so that it has to adapt to these changes, and thus, you get a stronger and more resilient plant as a result. This stronger plant results because when cannabis plants grow on their own in the wild, they want to reach their top bud as high as they can. However, when you are growing cannabis for commercial purposes, you do not want just one large and tall bud, but many, many buds. This part is where training comes in. The natural method of growth does not allow the buds on the bottom of the plant to get as much light as they need, so by training the plant, you also allow the plant to have evenly healthy buds instead of the healthiest buds at the top of the plant and the buds at the bottom suffering more. There are to ways to train your plant: *High-Stress Training (or HST) and Low-Stress Training (or LST).*

Loss Stress Training (LST)

Low-Stress Training is a method that is best for plants growing in indoor gardens and exposed to light sources for growth. LST can increase your yield greatly. We usually use this method in the vegetative state, but you can sometimes also do it during the flowering stage. LST involves influencing the direction and method of growth that your plant wants to create naturally. For example, if you see that one branch is becoming much too tall, to avoid growing an uneven plant with uneven buds, you will tie this long branch down so that it does not continue to outgrow the rest of the branches. You can also tie down the plant's top branch so that it does not grow too big and shade the rest of your plant. Doing this allows the chemicals running up and down the stem and branches to be spread out more evenly throughout the plant, leading to more even growth of the branches and buds and more even growth of the overall plant. To accomplish this, use plant-specific tape designed with the health of the plant in mind.

When you properly train your plant in this way, many branches grow around the pot that the plant is in. Then, when the buds grow, they grow at an even level to each other, letting them all get the right amount of light without being shaded by other areas of the plant that are covering them. One other way to accomplish this type of training is to use a screen placed above the plant to act as a sort of barrier of growth. When a branch grows through the screen, you can bend it and send it back down into the screen so that it continues to grow in a downward fashion. One other LST method that can be useful but that is a little more invasive is to bend the branches of the plant in certain places so that it kinks and then begins to grow in a downward fashion. This method is called *Stem Mutilation or Super Cropping.* You do not want to snap the branch; you just want to put a kink in it so that it stays bent. If you think you will snap the branch, try the following; before you bend it, begin rolling it between your fingers until it becomes softened, and then it should be able to kink much easier.

High-Stress Training (HST)

High-Stress Training is a great training method for plants that are growing outdoors and have more space to grow. This training method should be restricted o the vegetative stage of plant growth since it involves stressing the plant. Stressing the plant should not be done after the vegetative stage as it can interfere with the buds' growth, which is the most important part of the plant growth if you are growing it for use as marijuana. HST involves breaking off parts of the plant at the top. To do this method, you will look for the newest growth location at the very top of the plant and remove this portion. This process leads to the growth of four branches off the top of the plant instead of only one or two, which will lead the plant to grow out in a more even manner instead of growing taller than it is wide. This method can carry risks as it leaves your plant vulnerable to infection or disease as you are removing the topmost section of the plant. This method will be the most time consuming, so ensure that you have the time to devote to it.

High-Stress Training: Topping

There is one other method of High-Stress Training, which we call *Topping*. Topping is much simpler than the previous method as it does not involve any tools and is less risky. Topping involves removing a small part from the top of the plant with your fingernails. Doing this sends stress signals to the rest of the plant, promoting growth in the lower areas of the plant. This topping leads the plant to grow outward more than it grows upward, which allows the full plant to have access to sunlight instead of just the branches at the top of the plant. This method is to be done repeatedly throughout the vegetative stage of plant growth to promote the branches' lower growth throughout this stage.

Pruning

You can also *Prune* your plant to keep it potent and healthy. Pruning involves searching for areas of the plant that you determine will not receive adequate sunlight or nutrients because of the look of them or their location on the plant (i.e., in very shaded areas of the plant). You can remove these areas of the plant by snipping them off, allowing the plant to redirect its energy and resources to other areas of the plant to grow and flourish. Doing this will lead to maximum potency and the best parts of the plant getting what they need to grow and be strong.

The Vegetative Stage, Continued

At this stage, you can begin to examine your plant to determine different things about it. For example, you can look at the space between each of the nodes on your cannabis plant. The nodes are the parts of the plant where there are new stems containing leaves that jut out from the plant's main stem. If the space between the nodes is small and your plant is proving to grow densely in its leaf-spacing, you are growing an Indica strain of cannabis. If the node spacing is large and the plant is growing longer and more spread out, you are growing a Sativa strain of cannabis.

As the plant grows and grows, it is necessary to begin watering your plant more and more. When it is small, the watering should focus on the soil directly under the stem. As the plant grows in this stage, you can begin watering the plant at a wider circumference from the stem as the roots will have spread out underneath the soil. Doing this will ensure that the plant stays healthy and is taken care of in a well-rounded manner. Doing this will also allow the outermost roots to grow and develop, which will keep them spreading out and will allow the plant to grow and flourish.

At this stage, you can also begin using soil that contains some nutrients, especially nitrogen. As the plant grows and spreads, it will need more nutrients to stay strong and healthy. When the plant is young, this is not as necessary as it mostly requires water and air, but later on, in the process, it will begin needing food. This process is similar to a human baby beginning to eat solid food instead of just milk as it reaches its stages of rapid growth. Further, the plant needs many hours of sunlight per day at this stage as it will use this light to grow and develop. It needs 18 hours of sunlight per day.

Stage 5: Flowering

The flowering stage begins, as you can imagine when the buds begin to develop. When a plant is growing naturally in the wild, it will be affected by changing seasons, as this comes with changes in the amount of sunlight per day, the amount of water (in the form of rainfall), and the temperature outside. Naturally, this growth stage will coincide with a reduction in the amount of sunlight that the plant is exposed to in a day from about 18 hours to around 12 hours. Naturally, this stage would occur at the end of the summer as the days begin to shorten.

You will need to change the amount of light you are exposing your plants to at this stage. You will need to do this to induce flowering if you are growing your cannabis plant in one of the following situations; indoors, in a controlled environment, at a time of year when plants would not normally bloom or in an environment when plants could not normally bloom.

This stage is likely the stage when you will feel most rewarded as you will be able to begin seeing the fruits of your labor coming to fruition.

At this stage can begin to look for signs that will tell you the sex of your plants. Doing this is necessary so that you can control the pollination of your plants. You need to determine so you can decide whether or not you want your female plants to get pollinated- as they will die shortly after that. Many people who grow cannabis in a controlled environment will determine the sex of their plants and then separate the males from the females for this reason.

You do not want to prune your plants any time after this stage of growth, as it will disturb your mature plant's natural growth and disrupt the hormones in your plants, which can lead to plant growth complications. You will also need to support your plant's buds as they can weigh down the stems, which could eventually lead to the stem snapping. To avoid this, you will need to trellis your buds. Trellising your buds means that you can support your plants using wire or wooden rods that the stems and buds can grow around so that the plant's stems do not fully support their weight. At this stage, you also want to continue to feed your plants with nutrients so that they continue to grow strong and healthy, especially in this flowering stage.

Your buds will begin to grow the most rapidly at the end of this plant growth phase, near the sixth or seventh week. At the beginning of the flowering phase, you will not notice too much bud growth, but as this phase progresses, your buds' growth will increase exponentially. Then, the buds' growth will slow down again at the end of this phase, which marks the end of the cannabis plant growth cycle. At this point, the buds will be fully grown and formed to their mature size and shape. When the buds become fully matured (at the end of this phase), your buds will be ready to be harvested and then eventually sold, smoked, or whatever else you plan to do with them.

Stage 6: Determining Maturity and the Harvest Stage

When it comes time to harvest your plants, there are some different options available to you. Your first step is deciding whether your plants are ready to harvest.

To determine whether your plant is ready to harvest, you can do so by examining some specific areas of your plant. You can usually do this around the end of the flowering phase when you determine that your buds are mature enough.

To determine this, you will first look at the stigma of your plants. The stigma is those small female sex organs used to attract the pollen released by the male plants. You will need to be examining the stigma on your plant throughout the flowering phase so that you will be able to determine when they have reached full maturity.

The stigma will initially be white, but as the growth progresses and matures, you will see them turn to an orange color instead.

The second thing you can look for is the *Trichomes* of your cannabis plant. The trichomes are those small crystal-like structures on the buds and the leaves of the marijuana plant. They are sticky in texture and are the part of the plant that gives each strain its characteristic scent that you have likely grown to love. The word "trichome" means "Fine Outgrowth" which tells us what they are on the plant. In the trichomes, you will be able to find the most information about whether your plant is ready for harvest or not. To determine this with the most accuracy, you will need a small handheld microscope that you can likely buy from any plant store in your area. You need this because you will need to observe the trichomes' color, which can only be seen with accuracy very close up, and you cannot determine this with the naked eye. You can use this microscope to observe the changes in the trichomes' color throughout the flowering stage so that when your buds have matured, you can examine the trichomes and see if your plant is ready for harvest.

In the beginning, the trichomes of the plant will be clear in color. You will see them transition to an opaque shade, which indicates the maximum THC potency levels. At this point, they will have reached the maximum potency (in terms of THC content).

As the trichomes break down during the progression of the plant's progression, this results in a chemical called *Cannabinol* getting produced, which is one reason why the plant comes with so many pain-relieving benefits as well as insomnia and inflammation. This chemical does not lead to a feeling of being high; however, that is the THC. At this point, you will then see them transition to an amber shade.

Once you determine that your plants are mature enough to be harvested, you can begin to plan for your next stages.

Cultivation and Curing

Once you have determined that your plants are ready to be harvested, the next step that you will need to take is to dry the buds so that they are ready to be consumed in whatever way you wish to consume them.

The best and most effective way to dry your cannabis buds is thorough a process called *curing.* This process is a process of drying that occurs over an extended period. There are a few reasons why curing is the best option for drying your buds.

The first reason is that it increases the potency of your cannabis buds. Once you harvest your buds, they do not stop their maturity; in fact, they will continue to increase in potency for some time if you dry them through the slower curing process. They will continue to increase in potency as the buds' non-psychoactive chemicals will get converted to THC over time, making the THC content stronger.

If you choose to dry your buds quickly and in higher temperatures, the quality of the smell of your buds will decrease. Many people find that one of the best qualities of cannabis is the smell of the buds, and many people turn to this quality to determine their preference for choosing a strain. If you cure your buds at lower temperatures over time, you will maintain the strong scent of the cannabis that so many people look for.

Further curing your cannabis buds will help them to last longer in storage without going moldy or stale. This benefit is because they will have fully dried out over a long period, allowing you to keep them stored in an airtight container for up to two years without having them go bad.

You may now be wondering how you can cure your cannabis buds. While there are many methods for doing this, the simplest and most popular method is to cure them at a temperature of 60 to 70 degrees Fahrenheit in a dark room. You will also want to keep the humidity levels at about 50%.

First, you will cut off branches of your cannabis plant that are about 12 to 16 inches in length. You will then take off any leaves that you do not need or that are in the way of your buds. Then, you will hang these branches upside down by attaching them to a string or a line of wire. Doing this will allow you to leave them to cure over time. You will then set up a fan in the same room to help you circulate the air around the room.

You will leave them in these conditions until you notice the following; Check the leaves of the branches that you have hung up, and when they snap upon being bent (rather than simply folding over), then your plants are almost fully cured. Curing could take somewhere between 5 and 15 days. When you notice that your plants are at this point, you will then remove the branches' buds.

Once you remove the buds, do not throw away the leaves. The next step is to place the buds in some type of airtight container. In this container with the buds, you will place the leaves. The purpose of this is to allow the outer layers of the buds to absorb the moisture content within the leaves. Letting this process happen will make your buds presentable and aromatic. You will do this for the first 4 to 8 weeks of the life of your cannabis plant. For the first week, ensure that you open the container to allow the buds to get some air at least a couple of times per day. For the second and third week, you can reduce this to once per day. In the third week, your buds are theoretically ready to be used, but leaving them for an additional 4 to 5 weeks will result in a very successful curing process. Whether you have the time for this or not will depend on the purposes you are growing your cannabis and whether you have the patience to wait the extra few weeks.

Chapter 7: How to Maintain Your Plants

In this chapter, we will look at what you need to do to maintain your indoor cannabis growing system.

Properly maintaining your garden will help you to get the highest yield possible and keep your plants healthy and thriving in their growing environment. Depending on what type of growing system you choose, there are different ways to maintain your plants based on your chosen system. However, you should always follow a general set of rules to achieve the right amount of pH, temperature levels and prevent things like pests and disease. I will be walking you through all the necessary maintenance for your hydroponic system so you can prevent anything bad from happening to your plants.

What Maintenance Needs To Be Done?

There are six areas of maintenance that you constantly need to be looking out for in your indoor growing system. None of these tasks are exciting at the least, which generally gets given the least attention. Everybody loves to maintain the plants, grow beds, and their garden, but they often leave their reservoir's actual maintenance as an afterthought. Although a little bit boring, your reservoir is a huge aspect of your system, so not properly maintaining it can cause death to all your plants in the worst-case scenario. Let's take a look at the six areas you need to maintain frequently:

1. Maintain Ideal Nutrient Temperatures

You ALWAYS need to keep your water/nutrient solution at a temperature of 65 to 75 degrees Fahrenheit. If temperatures exceed 75 degrees, the oxygen levels are at risk of decreasing, which will create the ideal environment for root rot to grow. On the other hand, low temperatures will cause the plant to grow slowly. If you have a small reservoir, you can use aquarium heaters to warm up your nutrient solution. You may require a stronger heater if your reservoir is quite large. When it comes to your solution becoming too warm, you can cool your nutrient solution in these following ways:

- Use a reservoir chiller

The easiest solution to cool down a warm nutrient solution is to use a water chiller. These chillers will help you run your nutrient solution through a cold coil, which will cool down its temperature. There are some DIY options for this, but water chillers are much better as they are accurate and lets you choose your ideal temperature for your solution to be at and can help you keep at a constant temperature. This piece of equipment varies in price depending on how big your reservoir is like the bigger it is; you require a more powerful chiller.

- Keep your reservoir in the shade.

A cheap way to keep your nutrient solution is cool is to build some sort of cover to help keep the temperature cool. You can use shade cloth or build a box that can cover your solution. Doing this will also help keep the sun away as some plants thrive well with too much direct sunlight.

- Add ice to your reservoir.

A cost-effective alternative to cooling down your reservoir is to add ice into your nutrient solution. The easiest way to do this is to freeze your ice by filling up a jar with water and freezing it, then you can add it to your reservoir. You have to keep in mind that you don't want to cool your solution too quickly or too much as that can harm your plants. Make ice blocks/cubes of different sizes so you can control the amount of extra water and temperature change that you're giving to your solution.

- Change the color of your reservoir.

If your reservoir is a darker color, it is likely to hold more heat compared to a reservoir that is of a lighter color. A good way to get rid of some heat is to paint your reservoir into a lighter color like white. Doing this can help you lower the temperature of your solution by a few degrees. If you don't want to paint your reservoir, you can simply wrap it in mylar or foil as metallic will help deflect some heat away.

- Top your reservoir off with cold water

If your solution increases in temperature on a warm day, simply add some cool water into your solution. Doing this is likely the easiest way to lower the temperature quickly. Do keep in mind if you are using this method to top up your solution as it will likely dilute due to the extra water you added.

- Bury your reservoir underground

If your hydroponic system is outside, you can simply bury your reservoir underground with some soil. The natural ground will keep your reservoir cool by keeping it away from direct sunlight. Doing it this way is also a very cheap option but will require more manual labor.

2. Top Off Your Hydroponic Reservoir

If you are using a circulating hydroponic system, you need to make sure you are topping off your reservoir when changing the solution. You will lose a lot of water due to plant processes and evaporation, so you will need to keep replacing the water to keep it running smoothly. The smaller your reservoir is, the more often it will need to be topped up.

3. Change Your Water

Depending on which hydroponic system you chose to use, you will need to change your solution based on that. There are many different and conflicting opinions out in the market, so it'll be hard for you to find one answer for this. In my opinion, I find that changing your nutrient solution every two weeks is ideal for your plants. If you want to be more accurate, you can purchase an EC meter to analyze how much fertilizer is currently in your water. However, it won't tell you the amounts of each nutrient in there. Plants do not absorb every nutrient at the same rate, so topping up too much of one nutrient can also harm it. Water refreshes will allow you to ensure that your solution is well-balanced in the nutrient that it contains. Doing this will help you achieve less build up in your system, a good chemical balance and will allow you to clean your entire reservoir.

4. Provide Proper Oxygen Levels

To achieve healthy root growth in your plants, you need to have a well-oxygenated nutrient solution. This kind of solution is an absolute must for your plant to grow and helps with the growth of beneficial organisms that will strengthen your overall plant. You can also add an extra air stone, which will help your solution to maintain a higher level of dissolved oxygen.

5. Keep the Filter Clean

Adding a filter into your hydroponic system is always a good idea. What this does is it will prevent things like debris and plant matter from wandering into your reservoir. If you clean the filter often, you can reduce the amount of build-up which may attract pests. However, if you are using a DWC system (deep water culture), you don't need to use a filter as debris will typically float to the top of the solution. However, you do need to clean that debris out.

6. Conduct Regular EC and pH Checks

I mentioned earlier in this book about the importance of maintaining proper pH levels. Keeping tabs on your pH and EC levels are crucial when it comes to maintaining your reservoir. Your pH should ALWAYS be within the 5.5 to 6.5 range. In terms of EC, this will vary based on the plant you are looking to grow. Do some of your research specific to the plant you will grow and find out what EC levels are best for your garden and keep maintaining it at that level.

7. Conduct Regular Equipment Checks

Regularly checking the functionality of your equipment is always a good idea. Things like broken aerators, pumps, and connections typically go unnoticed, causing harm to your or preventing them from growing. If you can, keep spare parts around for backup to help prevent any long-lasting damage if a certain part breaks down at an inopportune time.

Maintain Proper Lighting CyclesLighting is very important, and it can have a large effect on your plants in the long run. The timing you set for your light/dark cycle is extremely important when you are growing a plant indoors, as there is no natural cycle like there would be outside with the sun. Ideally, your lights need to be on for 16 – 20 hours over 24 hours during the vegetative growth stage. You will then need to switch over to 12 hours of light per 24 hours during the time you want them to bloom. You will need to turn your lights on and off at the same time every day; otherwise, you may stress out your plants. Having a timer is essential for indoor growth. You can use your timer for your exhaust fan as well, but it is easier to just spend a couple of extra dollars on a thermostat switch.

Chapter 8: How to Overcome Challenges

This chapter will learn about several of the most common challenges you will face when growing marijuana indoors. We will spend most of this chapter talking about pests and diseases, and we will finish with the topic of challenges related to legality.

Introduction to Pests and Disease

The best way to prevent pests and diseases in any of your plants is to get familiar with the most common ones. By understanding what they are and the environments they typically like, you can prevent it from happening rather than fix it every time.

Typically, it should be very easy to identify what is happening to your plant as long as you have existing knowledge of it. If you don't, the signs and symptoms are likely to go unnoticed until your plant starts to die. Let's first take a look at the most common pests:

Common Pests

1. Spider Mites

Spider mites are the most common and annoying of all indoor plant pests. They are small bugs that are less than 1mm in length. Technically, they are in the arachnid family, and because of their small size, many people don't notice that they have them until your plants are very damaged. To fix this problem, you need to spot them before they do too much damage. You can do this by looking for webbing; if there is webbing, you may have a case of spider mites. Another way to identify this is to grab a tissue and wipe the underside of your plant leaves. If you notice your tissue comes out streaked with spider mite blood, then you 100% have the spider mites.

2. Thrips

Thrips are tiny bugs that are around 5mm in length. They are a bit harder to identify, but their damage is quite obvious if they are there. Look at your plant leaves' tops and see if you can see any small metallic black specks. You may notice that your plant leaves are starting to dry out and turn brown if there are. There also may be some yellowish-brown spots. These spots come up because the thrips are sucking the leaves dry of their moisture.

3. Aphids

Aphids are also commonly known as plant lice. They can be gray, green, or black. It does not matter what color the aphids are; they all do the same damage to plants. They typically like to suck all the moisture and juice out of plant leaves, which turns them yellow. They typically will gather at the stem of your plant, but you can find them anywhere. Check out the stem first if you suspect that you have an aphid infestation.

4. Whiteflies

Whiteflies are flies that look like white moths and are about 1mm in length. Since they are white, it makes them pretty easy to spot, but they are difficult to get rid of as they will fly away pretty quickly if the plant is disturbed. They also like to suck all the plants' moisture, which will cause your plants to have some yellowing and white spots.

5. Fungus gnats

Did you know that adult fungus gnats aren't harmful? However, their larvae will eat your feeder roots and roots, which will slow down your plant's growth. These gnats will also cause bacterial infection and could lead to plant death.

Remember that the best way to fix your pest problems is to prevent them in the first place. Later on in this chapter, I will teach you prevention measures after we discuss the most common plant diseases.

Common Diseases

Now, let's take a look at some of the most common indoor plant diseases. Understanding these will help you quickly identify them when it happens so you can help your plants recover as fast as possible.

1. Powdery Mildew

If your plants look like somebody had sprinkled white powder all over your stems and leaves, then you probably have powdery mildew. If you leave this untreated, it will stunt your plant growth, causing yellowing of plant tissues and leaf drops. If your plant is left untreated for a long time, it will die.

2. Downy Mildew

Downy mildew and powdery mildew are different, so don't get these two confused. While powdery mildew causes your plants to have white powder all over your stems and leaves, downy mildew will mostly show up on the underside of your leaves. This mildew doesn't look as powdery as powdery mildew does, but both of these will cause your plant leaves to turn yellow. Just remember, if the white powder appears on the underside, it is likely downy mildew, whereas if the powder appears on the stems, it's likely powdery mildew.

3. Gray Mold

Gray mold is also known as ghost spot or ash mold. To identify this disease, look for fuzzy gray abrasions that typically start as little gray spots on your leaves. You will notice that these spots continue to deteriorate until your plant turns mushy and brown.

4. Root Rot

If your plants are being given too many waters with pathogens in it, root rot will happen. We talked about this earlier in the book, so maintaining proper levels in your hydroponic medium is crucial. When this happens, your plants will begin to wilt and turn yellow. You will notice that the roots will get mushy as well.

5. Iron Deficiency

If your plants lack iron, it means that they also lack chlorophyll. You can tell this by looking at the leaves when the leaves turn into a bright yellow color while the veins remain green, it is a sign of an iron deficiency. This disease is often improperly diagnosed as another disease when simply your plant is just lacking some iron.

How to Prevent and Control Pests

You likely know by now that gardening comes with its challenges, as there are many factors involved. One of these factors includes pests and disease, which could plague your plant when you least expect it. In this section, we will look at how you can prevent pests and disease in your hydroponic garden so that you end up with the biggest and healthiest yield possible. Now that you know the most common pests that your plants could be facing, we will look at what you can do to prevent this.

As I briefly mentioned, the number one factor that will help keep your garden healthy and pest-free are to prevent the chances of pests wanting to inhabit your garden in the firsts place. By taking the appropriate steps to make your garden an environment that pests want to stay away from, you will give yourself the best chance for a healthy and thriving hydroponic garden. We will look at what these preventative measures are below. We will begin by talking about pests. Specific to the pests that I mentioned earlier in this chapter, you can do a few things to help control and prevent their appearance in the first place.

- Sticky Traps

Firstly, you can use sticky traps. You have probably seen these traps in your lifetime before, as they are commonly used to trap house flies. You can also choose different colored traps to help you better identify which pests you are catching. For instance, yellow card sticky traps will attract whiteflies and fungus gnats, while blue card sticky traps attract thrips. When using this method, be sure to place some traps at a low level and others at a medium level in terms of your plant height. These locations are where the fungus gnats like to congregate, giving you the best chance of catching them.

- Pest Sprays or Pesticides

You can also use different sprays to get rid of these pests but be sure to avoid chemicals like *Eagle* or *Avid*. This point is especially important if you are growing plants that you later plan to eat or ingest in some form-like cannabis. Try to choose organic sprays if possible. Alternatively, many people like to make organic pesticides themselves. These are especially beneficial if you are growing vegetables or if you are against the use of pesticides. Some common homemade pest sprays include the following;

Many people choose to make a spray consisting of Himalayan pink salt and water to deal with spider mites, which they then spray on the plants.

You can make another popular natural homemade pesticide from 1 ounce of garlic and one medium onion mixed with 1 quart of water, left for one hour to infuse. Then, 1 tsp of cayenne pepper and1 tbsp of liquid Castile soap (or vegetable soap). This solution can then be sprayed on your plants to get rid of a wide variety of pests without harming the plants or vegetables themselves.

Arguably the most well-known natural pesticide is called *Neem*. This pesticide has been used for years by aboriginals to keep pests of all sorts away. This pesticide gets its name from the leaf of a tree, and you will need to get your hands on oil from this tree leaf to make it, though it should not be hard to find due to its popularity. This pesticide is very powerful while also being completely natural, making it the top choice for many. To make this, you will need to mix a one-half ounce of Neem oil with one-half teaspoon of organic soap liquid and two quarts of water (warm). You can then spray this on your plants without harming them, and this will keep pests away.

- Beneficial Predators

Lastly, you can use beneficial predators to kill pests that appear on your plants. One example of these beneficial predators is *Nematodes*. Nematodes are more commonly known as roundworms. These beneficial predators can help treat pests such as gnats, caterpillars, grubs, crane flies, thrips, ants, moths, and fly larvae. One of the benefits of using these beneficial predators to treat your plants is that they will not harm you or your plants, and there is no risk of putting too many of them in your garden. This benefit means that they will be able to eradicate a pest problem or prevent it in the first place, without risking your plants themselves.

How to Prevent and Control Diseases

Once again, the number one factor that will help to keep your garden healthy is preventing the chances of diseases wanting to grow or inhabit your garden in the firsts place. Making your garden environment uninhabitable to diseases like mold or fungus will keep your plants healthy.

A good idea for your grow room is always to ensure a constant, light breeze is present, as this will strengthen the stems of your plants and help you create an environment that is less hospitable for flying pests and mold. You can use a wall-mounted circulating fan for this. Make sure to prevent windburn of your plants by not pointing your fans directly at your plants.

Before you begin growing anything or introducing plants into your garden, ensure that your garden's entire apparatus and other components are sterilized and disinfected. You can do this by using a ten percent peroxide solution to disinfect everything before you begin gardening.

Preventing pests and diseases is much better than trying to fix your plants after the fact. First of all, wear clean clothes before going into your grow room. Many diseases and pests could be on your clothes from the outside world and easily make a new home in your plants. Ensure that you are wearing indoor shoes that haven't touched the outside world to prevent bringing in any outdoor pests or diseases. Next, make sure you are keeping your grow area clean by cleaning up any spills or accidents. Many types of mildew and mold come about due to excess humidity and water, so ensuring that you have clean water is the best way to prevent these nasty molds from growing. Lastly, keep your plants as clean as possible. If you come across any dead plant matter near your grow area, pick it up. Be sure that you are also pruning your plants whenever necessary to remove dead/diseased leaves and branches. Reducing the amount of dead plant matter reduces the risk of getting any pests or diseases.

Keeping your plants as healthy as possible is another great way to fight off diseases and pests. For this reason, carefully choosing the best nutrients to use for your plant is important. For instance, make sure you are always keeping tabs on your plant's pH levels; the more optimal your pH levels are, the better your plants can fight off any diseases and pests. Be sure to also do some research on the best nutrients for the type of medium you plan to use. If you plan on using coco coir as your hydroponic medium, then look to purchase coco-coir specific nutrients. Since coco coir binds with magnesium and iron, your plant can easily become starved of those nutrients because the base won't contain the optimal amounts.

Moreover, giving your plants supplements will also keep them healthy. Rhino Skin is a supplement that is a soluble potassium silicate formulation that will help to strengthen your plants physically. Essentially, it strengthens your plant's cell walls and helps protect your plants from disease, drought, heat, and other possible stressors.

Challenges Related to Legality

In this section, we will discuss a challenge that you may face depending on where you live. We will talk about the legality and how this will affect your marijuana growth.

Marijuana is a plant that comes with a deep history, and it is still, to this day, a heavily debated topic of discussion. This plant has endless possibilities and uses, and it is widely used and discussed across the world because of this. There are many debates about whether it should be legal to grow, sell, and consume it due to its numerous benefits outside of getting people high. There is still a long way to go when it comes to this plant, but if you are lucky enough to live in a location where growing marijuana is legal, you will not have as much to consider.

After the War on Drugs began in 1970, a report two years later mentioned that marijuana might not be the evil drug that it appeared to be two years prior. This report was put forth by the National Commission on Marijuana and Drug Abuse, and it deemed marijuana as a misunderstood drug. This report stated the recommendation for less severe sentences related to the possession or the sale of marijuana. The president ignored this report, and the War on Drugs continued.

These laws remained in place until California decided to make a change for the first time since 1970. The state of California put forth the Compassionate Use Act in 1996, which decriminalized the use of marijuana by those who wished to use it to deal with chronic disease and illness. Following this, 26 other states and Washington, D.C., and Puerto Rico and Guam (which are territories of the USA), also legalized marijuana use for people with chronic and severe illnesses. This law remained so until several states began to decriminalize the use of marijuana for recreational purposes. The first states to amend this law were Washington and Colorado, who made this change in 2012. As of now, there are 11 states in which people can use marijuana for recreational purposes legally. These states are listed below for your reference.

- Washington
- Maine
- Illinois
- Nevada
- Colorado
- Michigan
- Massachusetts
- Alaska
- Vermont
- Oregon
- California

The effects of marijuana legalization are clear from a global perspective. With a new marijuana legalization movement across the world, many countries like Canada and the United States have been fighting to legalize and decriminalize marijuana. This movement had brought in millions of tax dollars to Canada already since the legalization in April 2019. Since legalization in Canada, we have already seen a severe decline in alcohol purchases. With many other countries that will be following Canada's lead, we can begin to see the effects of marijuana legalization globally.

Locations Where We Can Observe This

The following places around the world allow the recreational use of marijuana.

- Peru.

Peru allows the possession and the consumption of recreational marijuana as long as the person consumes it immediately.

- Spain

Spain allows its citizens to grow and consume marijuana in their private dwellings. It is not legal to sell marijuana, but it is very easy to access it as the laws are not very strict as there are several private "cannabis clubs" where you can access it once you gain entry. This entry does not require much, just signing on a dotted line.

- The Netherlands

The Netherlands has not technically legalized marijuana yet, but similar to Spain, the laws are not very strict regarding enforcement. This law works in more of a "don't ask, don't tell" sort of format. The sale of marijuana is deemed illegal, but the government does not punish people as long as it does not harm society or its people. The sale of marijuana is only allowed past when sold to citizens of the Netherlands, except in Amsterdam, which is well-known for its loose marijuana laws and marijuana cafes.

- South Africa

South Africa very recently rules marijuana sales and consumption legal. It is also legal to grow marijuana for personal use.

- Canada

Canada is the second country to legalize marijuana nationwide and the largest country to do so. Canada legalized marijuana for recreational use in 2019.

- Uruguay

Uruguay legalized marijuana nationwide in 2012, making it the first country to legalize marijuana across the entire country at once.

The Future Of Marijuana Legalization

In the future, many more countries may be looking to liberalize marijuana. Countries like Thailand, who historically has a strict ban on marijuana, are in talks of legalizing medicinal marijuana. This progress is a huge step forward in countries that are known to be more conservative than liberal. Suppose we extrapolate from the marijuana movement that has happened already. In that case, we are likely to see a continued growth in dispensaries and cafes that will offer more and more marijuana products.

Chapter 9: Common
Mistakes to Avoid

When you begin anything new, you will likely make mistakes. These mistakes will teach you as you go, but it can be devastating to make a mistake that can cost you your entire crop when it comes to indoor gardening. In this chapter, we will discuss several of the most common mistakes made by beginners so that you can learn from the mistakes of others instead of having to go through them yourself.

Tips for Your First Time Growing Marijuana Indoors

If this is the first time you are growing plants indoors and in a hydroponic system, you have to set up the right space to do it. This space doesn't need to be a typical looking grow 'room' like the ones you see in movies. It can simply be a spare room, a cabinet, tent, closet, or the corner of your basement. The most important part is to tailor your equipment and the plants you choose to fit the space. This consideration is why choosing the right indoor plant is important as some plants grow too large for a small tent.

For your first project, you ideally want to start with a smaller plant in a smaller place. The smaller your growth, the less expensive it will be for you to complete your project. It is also way simpler to watch over just a few plants rather than a large amount of them. Also, smaller grows, in the beginning, will be less costly for you if you do end up making mistakes. Keep in mind that many novice plant growers will experience obstacles like losing a plant to disease or pests. If you are trying to grow ten plants at once in your first grow, you may end up losing a lot of money if they are unsuccessful, whereas if you started with just 1 – 2 plants, it wouldn't hurt your wallet as much. Although we are trying to keep your growth area small, we must also think big simultaneously. When you are designing and creating you grow space, make sure to account for the room that the equipment will need like fans, ducting, lights, and the room that the plants will take up. If your grow room is somewhere quite small, like a closet, tent, or cabinet, you can choose to open the door or the entrance and take out your plants when working with them for ease of access. If this is not possible, make sure you are accounting for the room you will need to take up to care for your plants physically.

Next, make sure you are maintaining cleanliness. This point is especially important when you are growing your plant indoors. Ensure you are frequently sanitizing your workspace and avoiding growing your plants on raw wood, drapes, or carpeting as these types of spaces are difficult to clean. Another important part of your grow space is to ensure that your light is sealed tight. If you leak light during dark periods, it can confuse your plant as it will complicate the imitation of the sun's light and dark cycles that you are trying to emulate. This necessary point is why I recommend that you put it in a sealed closet or a tent that you can zip up to keep the growing environment dark when need be.

Further, you should ensure that your grow space is placed in a convenient spot as you will need to monitor your plants often and carefully. It is important to check in on your plant every day, and if you are a beginner, you probably would like to check in multiple times in a day until you're sure you finish everything you needed to do. If your grow space is in an inconvenient area like in a separate building, it may prevent you from being able to check in on your plant multiple times per day. Additionally, you have to maintain optimal temperature and humidity in your grow space. If your space is humid or warm, you may face more obstacles related to grow-space control. Choose a dry and cool area with plenty of fresh air for your plants.

Improper Nutrient Levels

One major mistake that beginners often make is turning to a traditional fertilizer found at your nearest nursery. The problem here is that these are often made for soil-based gardens and not hydroponic systems. To ensure that your plants benefit from the nutrients you are giving them, you must ensure that these nutrients are fully dissolving in the water to create a nutrient-rich solution. If they simply sink to the bottom and refuse to dissolve, they will not reach your plants through the roots, and your plants will then likely suffer from a lack of nutrition.

pH Errors

When growing crops in a hydroponic system, your system's pH is very important as your plants will need to be provided with very specific pH ranges to grow and remain healthy and alive. The nutrient solution that you give your plants needs to be at the optimal pH for those specific plants to avoid living in an environment that is too acidic or too basic for them. To avoid this mistake, ensure that you know the pH level that your plants need to remain at. Then, you will need to have some way to measure the pH of your solution. You can do this with a pH meter or with pH testing strips. You will need to test your solution's pH once per day at minimum, if not more. If you are new to hydroponic gardening, you may wish to check this more often to ensure that you are on the right track until you get more comfortable with it.

Overfeeding

In most cases, overfeeding your plants is worse than underfeeding them. Once you have gained more experience with feeding your plants, you will slowly learn how to 'read' your plants for signs of excess nutrients or nutrient deficiencies.

Lighting Mishaps

As you know, by this point, lighting is one of the most important factors present in your hydroponic garden, next to the pH level. If you are going to choose one place to invest the most money, choose good quality lighting. Without the correct lighting schedules or the right types of lightbulbs, your plants could have difficulty growing. Ensure that you know the specific lighting schedule and type of lighting that your plants need and then make sure that you are giving them exactly what they need in terms of light quality and duration. Keep in mind that light streaming through a window is not enough to provide your plants with the light they need to grow strong and healthy.

Chapter 10:
Cloning Your Plants

The final stage of cannabis growth is called cloning. This chapter will learn about the cloning stage in detail, as it is one of the most important and interesting stages of the cannabis plant life cycle.

The Importance of Cloning Your Plants

The cloning stage of cannabis plant growth presents an alternative to growing your cannabis plant from seeds. If you began with seeds, this could prevent you from using seeds again if you want to continue growing more plants. For this reason, this stage could arguably be the first step in the cannabis plant life cycle, as it can begin the growth of a new plant. This fact demonstrates why the cannabis plant lives in a cycle, as it keeps going around and around again each time you grow new plants to maturity. If you wish to grow your plant in this way from here forward, this chapter will be of interest.

How to Clone Your Plants

Cloning is also known as *Asexual Reproduction. It* involves only one plant instead of the reproduction that we previously discussed, which combines the genetic material of two plants through pollination.

To clone a plant, you will use a razor which you will use to cut off a piece of your original plant. The plant which you wish to clone is called the *Mother Plant.* This plant is chosen for its health, the product it produces, and the ease with which it can grow since these characteristics will get passed onto the new plant in which you will grow through cloning. When cloning a plant, you want it to be somewhere around eight weeks into the vegetative stage of plant growth. This time is the opportune time for cloning. Before you are going to clone your plant, avoid giving it any fertilizer for a few days before cloning to prepare it. You will want to choose a lower branch on the stem, and then you will use your razor to cut off the branch at a forty-five-degree angle, as this gives you enough surface area for the new plant to grow new roots from. Once you cut them (do not use scissors as they are not sharp enough and will crush the stem), put the branch directly into the water. Putting them directly into the water will ensure that it stays fresh and that no air bubbles will be present inside the branch.

Once you do this, you will clip off the leaves to help induce this new small plant's growth. Halfway down the stem of the leaves, clip them off. After you have done this, you can plant your new clone. You can plant it in soil with no nutrients (it doesn't need them yet), in water alone, or Rockwool. Any of these three mediums will do.

Once you start to see roots growing on the bottom of your clone's stem, you will be able to plant them in whatever location you plan to have them grow from here forward. Then, you can continue the process of growth as you normally would from here on. This process is why we call it a plant life *cycle*; it goes around and around.

Once you have grown your first set of cannabis plants, you can determine which ones you want to clone so that your next set of plants will be as strong as possible. By choosing which plants you want to clone, you can ensure that your cannabis plant production improves with new plants' growth. For this reason, it is important to pay close attention to which of your plants sprouted the quickest, formed a seedling the quickest, and flowered the quickest. This information is an indication of a strong plant and a strong seed.

When it comes to commercial cannabis production, the farmers will usually plant all of the seeds and choose the best plant. When that ideal plant creates its seeds, the farmer will then clone those seeds to create a full harvest of ideal plants.

Conclusion

Thank you for reaching the end of this book; I hope it provided you with all of the information you need to grow beautiful, thriving marijuana plants indoors.

Now that you know how to begin your indoor marijuana garden, we will discuss what you should do once you harvest your plants. As you learned in this book, there are endless uses for marijuana. My essential advice is to know what you want to do with your finished product before growing your plants. For example, do you want to use them for smoking, for making edibles, for making vape oil? Whatever your intended use, knowing this before you begin, will help you to get the best possible finished product.

When you harvest your plants and dry the buds, you are ready to transform them into whatever you wish. If you want to make edibles, you can buy online tools that will help you transform the dried flower into THC oil. You can then use this oil for cooking. If you want to use the dried flower alone, you will need to make sure that you store it in a dark, cool, and dry place so that your marijuana stays fresh for as long as possible. Whatever you do, enjoy the process and enjoy your finished product.

Over the past few decades, marijuana has grown in popularity and has become decriminalized and legalized in numerous countries. With the marijuana liberalization movement, many people have become curious about this plant that offers so many healing properties.

As you can now understand, the history of marijuana is wrought with controversy. To this day, there are still many conflicting opinions on this plant. I hope that this book provided you with a deeper understanding of the many sides of the marijuana plant, including the medicinal properties it boasts, the ways that it can be used and benefitted from recreationally, and what the future of marijuana may hold. I also hope that this book opened your mind and helped you discover how you can benefit from this wonderful plant full of possibilities for anyone, no matter what they are looking to get out of it.

This book's purpose was to help you understand the basics of marijuana to learn to grow your marijuana plant most effectively and successfully. This book guided you through the history of marijuana, the science behind it, its effects, ways to use it, different strains of marijuana, its plant lifecycle, and things that you should know before you grow your plant to ensure its success.

Not only are there numerous uses for the marijuana plants that you grow using the information you have learned in this book, but it is also extremely fulfilling to raise your marijuana plants from seedling to harvest. You can use your marijuana plants for everything ranging from food to various therapeutic uses, as you learned. You will also be able to put your knowledge to the test by trying what you have learned in this book on your own. You can use the information contained within to grow a wide variety of different marijuana strains of your choice, depending on your intended uses and your preferences. The best way to improve your skills is to practice and to learn from your mistakes. I wish you success as you take on this journey, and I hope that you continue in your pursuit of the healthiest and most potent marijuana plants as you can grow.